WHEN EVERY MOMENT COUNTS

WHEN EVERY MOMENT COUNTS

WHAT YOU NEED TO KNOW ABOUT BIOTERRORISM FROM THE SENATE'S ONLY DOCTOR

SENATOR BILL FRIST, M.D.

ROWMAN & LITTLEFIELD PUBLISHERS, INC.
Lanham • Boulder • New York • Oxford

ROWMAN & LITTLEFIELD PUBLISHERS, INC.

Published in the United States of America
by Rowman & Littlefield Publishers, Inc.
4720 Boston Way, Lanham, Maryland 20706
www.rowmanlittlefield.com

12 Hid's Copse Road
Cumnor Hill, Oxford OX2 9JJ, England

British Library Cataloguing in Publication Information Available

Library of Congress Cataloging-in-Publication Data

Frist, William H.
   When every moment counts : what you need to know about bioterrorism
from the Senate's only doctor / Bill Frist.
      p. ; cm.
   ISBN 0-7425-2246-6 (pbk : alk. paper) — ISBN 0-7425-2245-8 (pbk. :
alk. paper)
   1. Bioterrorism—Popular works.
   [DNLM: 1. Anthrax—Popular Works.   2. Bioterrorism—Popular Works.
3. Anthrax Vaccines—Popular Works.   4. Biological Warfare—Popular
Works.   WC 305 F917w 2002]   I. Title.
   RC88.9.T47   F75   2002
   613.6—dc21   2001008752

Printed in the United States of America

CONTENTS

      INTERNET RESOURCES   173

      INDEX   175

      ABOUT THE AUTHOR   183

ACKNOWLEDGMENTS

This book would not have been possible without the help of many people who generously offered their expertise, wisdom, and encouragement along the way. To each and every one, my sincere and heartfelt thanks. While the responsibility for the contents of this book is mine alone, I will be forever grateful for the guidance, insights, and clarity so many individuals provided on this ever evolving and challenging field.

I would like especially to thank Ruth L. Berkelman, Michael Osterholm, Ken Bernard, Jerome "Jerry" M. Hauer, Robert S. Holzman, Bruce Gellin, Ali S. Khan, Allen S. Craig, Martin J. Blaser, Daniel R. Lucey, Gary J. Nabel, Reed V. Tuckson, Dean Ornish, William H. Roper, Stephanie Bailey, S. Ward Casscells, and John Morris.

For their help tracking down photographs that add to our understanding of the biological agents, I would like to thank Phil Robinson, Ruth Berkelman, Cristi Schwarcz, Eric Grafman, Steve Grosha, Christy Weishorn, Chuck Dasey, and Bryan Underwood.

Of course, there would have been no book without the support and encouragement of the Rowman & Littlefield Publishing Group. I would particularly like to thank Jed Lyons for his inspiration for the concept and whip-cracking to get it done on time. I appreciate most of all the superb research and writing assistance of Jack Croft.

Finally and most importantly, I thank Karyn and the boys, Bryan, Jonathan, and Harrison, who are my foundation in life.

INTRODUCTION

Are children at greater risk for certain types of bioterrorism than adults?

Should I be vaccinated against smallpox or anthrax?

What should I do if I find myself in the middle of a biological or chemical attack?

Should I buy a gas mask?

You will find the answers to these and more than 120 other questions in the chapters that follow. My purpose in writing this book is to help you be better equipped to protect yourself and your loved ones if a bioterrorist attack occurs in your community. You will discover how germs, when used by terrorists, might affect your life and the lives of your family members—and what you can do about it.

Everyone has concerns, and indeed many have real anxiety, in these times of heightened alert about potential terrorist activity in our communities. I've found that a little bit of information goes a long way in transforming that chronic and sometimes debilitating anxiety into a quiet, healthy resolve.

Bioterrorism is now a reality in the United States. Terrorists have used anthrax bacteria to infect, to kill, and to terrorize innocent people. In a sense, we were lucky: they could have used it as a weapon of mass destruction. Each of the biological agents I talk about in this book has been identified by our intelligence and public health experts as a potential bioterrorist weapon.

Since we as a nation are vulnerable to bioterrorism, it only makes sense that each of us does everything in our power to minimize our own vulnerabilities. The best way to begin to do that is to understand how viruses and bacteria might be used against us. My goal is to jump-start that process by concisely answering the questions and concerns, both conscious and unconscious, that we all have in these unusual times.

We learned much from the anthrax attacks in the fall of 2001. On October 4, just three weeks after the terrorist attacks on Washington, D.C., and New York City, we saw the first stories about the infection of a photo editor and, soon after, his coworker in Florida. A few days later, we heard about the infection of an NBC employee in New York. And on October 15, a letter laden with deadly anthrax was opened on Capitol Hill in the office of Senate Majority Leader Tom Daschle. Within days came the deaths of two Washington, D.C., postal workers.

We learned that every moment counts when terrorists turn a deadly biological agent into a weapon against us. We learned that viruses and bacteria can paralyze a community. We saw how conflicting messages about who is at risk, who should be taking antibiotics, and how mail should be handled all led to confusion, distrust, and even heightened fear, sometimes bordering on panic. Gaps in our public health system—the result of twenty years of neglect and underinvestment—became glaringly apparent. Our level of preparedness simply has not been what our nation deserves. Our government must address that level of preparedness, and the first steps are being taken (see chap. 11).

But the focus of this book is on you and what you need to know to be prepared.

Preparation against bioterrorism calls for a team approach. There can be no spectators. You are the key player. And being the key player means you have great responsibilities. Each of us is responsible for the safety and security of family members and loved ones. Each of us is responsible for demanding that our local governments provide for the security of our communities by creating a public health system that can respond quickly and efficiently.

Increased understanding of what is known today—even though, as we all have witnessed, this knowledge is changing rapidly—and what you can do to minimize the risk we now know exists can best be achieved by providing you and your family with as much basic, useful information as possible.

The format of this book is straightforward question and answer. The questions came from people like you, the reader. It's my hope that I cover not only the obvious questions we all have but also the questions that many of us just might not yet have thought of.

The perspective I bring to this book comes from my own experiences as a surgeon, senator, and parent. As a heart and lung transplant surgeon who routinely gave my patients strong immunosuppressive medicines that made them more susceptible to infections, I, by necessity, became a specialist in infectious diseases. As a U.S. senator, I have participated with my colleagues in the legislative response to improving our preparedness for, and response to, potential bioterrorist attacks. And as a husband and a parent of three teenage boys, I—like so many—look to my family's security as the most important thing in my life.

Everywhere I've gone—from school and church events with my own family, to public meetings and campaign appearances as a U.S. senator—I've been asked most of these questions many times. The answers are not the same as they were even a few months ago, and indeed the answers will change over time. This book addresses each question and provides the most up-to-date and accurate answer possible at the time of publication.

But our knowledge in this field changes daily, so no book can ever stay perfectly current. Given the limitations of the format, I've done my best to share what we know now, at the time of publication. However, methods of surveillance, diagnostic tests, and treatments are always improving. To help you keep up with changes as they inevitably develop, I have provided a list of what I consider to be some of the best, most useful, and most trusted Internet websites on bioterrorism.

This book, I hope, will be a useful and accessible reference to check something you heard at work, or on the television or radio, or in the coffee shop. My dream is to have the book sitting on your nightstand or maybe in your kitchen next to the telephone, available to answer that specific question that flies through your mind at any time of the day. I've discovered that television, because it is so transient, cannot provide this information in a way that you can access easily when you might need it. And the Internet, which I rely on extensively as a rapid and efficient communication tool, is just too disorganized for quick reference. Also, the integrity of the information you find on the Web is not always clear. So use this book as a ready reference.

I hope that you will want to read the book from cover to cover. Particularly, I urge everyone to read chapter 2, which focuses specifically on what you can do to reduce the vulnerabilities for yourself and your family. But I understand that many of you will want to skip around, focusing first on the answers to the questions you've already thought of.

You might want to glance through the questions on a particular biological agent that you've heard about or that is in the news. Or go straight to the index for the topics that interest you the most. Do glance at the photographs, just so you will have a visual impression of what these biological agents look like and some of the rashes they can cause. Sometimes just looking at the pictures helps reduce the mystery around these agents.

Most of all, I hope this book will serve as a useful and friendly reference for you and your family as we address the fact that our lives could be touched by this new form of terrorism. An informed family will be a family prepared.

1

ANTHRAX IN THE CAPITOL

Bioterrorism Hits Home

For two hours that morning, we talked about bioterrorism in hypothetical terms. Now, suddenly, it was all too real.

An Associated Press reporter asked me to respond to the news that a letter containing anthrax had been delivered to the Washington office of my colleague, Senate Majority Leader Tom Daschle. An undetermined number of staffers in Senator Daschle's Hart Senate Office Building suite had apparently been exposed to the potentially lethal biological agent when the letter was opened. President George W. Bush just minutes before had told the nation about the letter during informal remarks following an event at the White House.

I was stunned. I had spent the morning hosting a roundtable on bioterrorism at the Tennessee Emergency Management Agency headquarters in Nashville. I listened carefully as about three dozen doctors, nurses, hospital administrators, firefighters, police, and other law enforcement, public health, and emergency personnel from all across the state talked about how unprepared they were for the growing threat of bioterrorism.

Little did I know at the time that this initial press question would be my initiation into seven days that would severely test much of what we thought we knew about bioterrorism. Seven days that would challenge our fundamental clinical understanding of anthrax—how to diagnose it, how to treat it, how to protect those who may have been exposed—and how to communicate with the press and the public about a public health emergency with shifting facts and a fluid, rapidly evolving scientific knowledge base.

The coming week also would bring sharply into focus the vital role our public health system plays in responding to such an attack. After all, this was part of the first biological attack on U.S. soil involving anthrax and was only the second known biological attack in the United States in at least a century (the first, in 1984, involved salmonella poisoning of restaurant salad bars by a cult in Oregon).

The lessons learned from the abstract discussions in Nashville on Monday morning, October 15, 2001, would come alive and be played out in vivid detail in Washington over the next seven days.

MONDAY

As I prepared to host the bioterrorism roundtable in Nashville, a Florida man already had died of inhalational anthrax, and an assistant to *NBC News* anchor Tom Brokaw had been diagnosed with skin, or cutaneous, anthrax. An additional case of each form of the infectious disease would be confirmed later in the day.

So everyone in that room knew that the threat we once considered remote was growing. Frontline responders, those who will answer that panicky phone call or first see a person with symptoms, lacked appropriate training and protective equipment. State and county public health laboratories lacked adequately trained epidemiologists and state-of-the-art facilities and equipment. Community hospitals had no system to share information with each other or with local public health facilities in a timely way.

Vanderbilt Hospital—one of Tennessee's premier teaching and referral hospitals, where I had worked for nine years as a transplant surgeon before coming to the U.S. Senate—acknowledged that it did not have a bioterrorism preparedness plan in place and had not done training exercises to deal with this emerging threat. Nor had any of the community hospitals.

From rural doctors to city police and firefighters to state public health officials, all the way up to the governor's office, the story was the same: They just weren't prepared to respond to what might happen.

Following the conference, I walked into an adjacent room for a press briefing, and the question was no longer about what might happen. It was about what had already happened.

When asked about the Daschle letter, I simply replied that I was unaware of the report but that it would have to be confirmed. To be honest, I minimized it a bit in my own mind because I recalled receiving an anthrax hoax letter three years before. If the report was correct, this would be the first witnessed exposure of multiple people to the release of airborne anthrax.

My next scheduled stop was a speech about bioterrorism to the Nashville Rotary Club at a downtown restaurant. Ironically, I had picked the topic three weeks earlier when the meeting was booked, before anthrax was on anyone's radar screen.

By the time I arrived at the Rotary meeting, we had been notified that my own Public Health Subcommittee staff was on the same floor in the Hart building just down the hallway from where the letter had been opened. We were told that there was apparently a large amount of a powdery substance in the letter and that nasal swab testing and distribution of a short course of antibiotics had begun for those in the Daschle suite. I sensed that the issue was escalating.

I was able to get periodic progress reports by telephone from my subcommittee staff. At this point, the Hart building remained open and people were still at work at their desks. In fact, the building would stay open for another day and a half. The risk of exposure was unknown at the time.

I returned to Washington that afternoon and was asked by Senate Republican leader Trent Lott to be the liaison for the Republican senators to the fledgling medical and law enforcement investigation into the anthrax exposure at the Hart building.

Already, those within Senator Daschle's suite had been given nasal swab tests along with a three-day course of antibiotics. And a public health command room had been set up by Majority Leader Daschle in the secretary of the Senate's office on the third floor of the Capitol. It was in this room that data were reported and shared and strategies to deal with the evolving public health and environmental issues were discussed and developed.

Officials representing many agencies—the Centers for Disease Control and Prevention (CDC), the Capitol physician's office, the Defense Advanced Research Projects Agency (DARPA), the Senate sergeant at arms, the Capitol police, Senate leadership, the deputy surgeon general representing the Department of Health and Human Services, and the director of the District of Columbia health department—were almost always in that room for the next several days, coordinating among themselves and then reporting back to their home agencies.

To provide information to the Senate staff and the public at large, we held two press conferences on the first full day and then scheduled daily press conferences for the next week. But many staffers were still confused and anxious about their potential health risk.

Just a few doors from Senator Daschle's suite, my own health subcommittee staff members were experiencing firsthand the difficulty in obtaining helpful information during a public health emergency. Although they knew about the letter, primarily from press reports, almost nothing else was reaching them. Like the rest of the nation outside the walls of the building, their principal source of information was TV.

On that first day, staffers from Senator Daschle's offices turned to our health subcommittee staff with questions about anthrax and their own health risk, in part because they knew that my staff had been working on issues related to bioterrorism for a long time and in part because, as I am the Senate's only doctor, they knew that my staff and I are involved in most health-related issues. Is anthrax contagious? If I've been exposed, is my family at risk? However, no official word came from those conducting the investigation until later that afternoon, when a police officer visited my staff in the Hart building to confirm that a letter possibly laced with anthrax had been delivered to Senator Daschle's office.

In response, they were closing off a section of the Hart building. The officer would remain on duty outside my staff's door, but the primary reason was to ensure that the press did not bother them as they continued to work. Staffers moved in and out of that wing of the Hart building, totally unaware of any health concerns.

The ventilation system had been shut down within an hour of the incident to avoid potential spread of anthrax, and the staff was told to expect the offices to be warmer than usual. At that time, there was no discussion about their own health risk, and previous experience would suggest that they were not in harm's way.

Nasal swabs to determine how widespread exposure to the anthrax spores had been were eventually obtained from everyone in the Hart building. On Monday, only those present in the vicinity of the Daschle suite when the letter was opened were given preventive antibiotics pending results of the nasal swab tests.

When nasal swab test results confirmed the direct exposure to anthrax of twenty-eight people inside or immediately adjacent to the Daschle suite, anxiety across Capitol Hill soared. The innocent opening of a letter, a routine task that is done millions of times every day in offices across the country, suddenly escalated into a public health crisis that truly frightened many people who work on the Hill. Congressional mail was quarantined, and a month later, on November 16, 2001, a second anthrax-laced letter—this one addressed to Sen. Patrick Leahy—was discovered by government investigators.

Few of the office workers on that first day really understood what a positive nasal swab meant. What about those whose tests came back negative? Did they have anything to worry about? Why did some of them still have to take antibiotics? It seemed so confusing to everyone involved, including members of the press who were trying to interpret it all.

Anxiety was high. People were not getting the answers they needed. And it was only just beginning.

TUESDAY

Staff members who had continued working in their fifth- and sixth-floor Hart offices through Monday were surprised the next morning to find a police barricade barring the entrance to the southeast corridor. They were told that they could not return to their offices and were directed to obtain a nasal swab test and more information from the medical crew.

Hundreds and hundreds of concerned individuals lined up for the nasal swab tests in the Hart building. It was difficult for the necessary medical supplies to be maintained. Several times, the line stalled owing to lack of the antibiotic ciprofloxacin (Cipro) or the necessary sterile cotton swabs. Anyone who wanted testing simply had to show up; no one was turned away. Hundreds of people from all over Capitol Hill came to be tested, even if they were not in the Hart building. Many people showed up to be tested out of confusion, others out of fear.

Everyone receiving a nasal swab that day was given a three-day supply of Cipro and told to return for the test results; at that time they would be told whether they would have to take the antibiotics for sixty days. Because of all the confusion, misinformation floating around, and the fact that very little information was then being made available, my staff and I immediately went to work to make the official Senator Bill Frist website a central place where anyone could go to find accurate, up-to-date, pertinent information both on anthrax generally and on the rapidly evolving situation in the Senate office buildings.

It was not the first time my office had to deal with bioterrorism. Three years earlier, after I received the hoax letter labeled "ANTHRAX," I addressed with my staff mail-handling protocols for any letter that appeared suspicious. We were able to go back and find these protocols and post them immediately on the website so everyone had access to the information. We were among the first sites—even before the postal service—to have practical information on what to do if you received mail suspicious for anthrax.

Working with the Capitol physician and others involved in the situation, my staff gathered information from the command-room briefings and continually updated the postings. It was obvious that people were growing anxious for information about anthrax and developments on the Hill.

They tried to get on the CDC website, but it had crashed and no information was available on it. Where could they go to get information about their own personal health risk? Were the twenty-eight people who tested positive now infected with the most deadly form of anthrax disease, inhalational anthrax? (They weren't. The test merely confirmed that they had been exposed to the spores.) Why did some people around them have positive test results while their results were negative? How long would they be out of their offices? Should they go to work the next day?

People were desperate for information. And desperation can lead to frustration. And frustration can lead to anger. And they didn't know where to turn.

WEDNESDAY

Forty-eight hours after the anthrax-laced letter was opened, information was still scarce. Staff continued to show up for work, and the testing site was moved to the Russell Senate Office Building because the Hart building was closed.

As thousands of Senate and House staff and those who had been visiting Senate buildings on Monday lined up for their nasal swabs and three-day Cipro supply, my staff busily printed out information on anthrax exposure that we gathered from my Senate website and others and handed it out to those who waited in line. They were understandably eager for information.

The Senate and House leadership met early Wednesday morning and received reports that environmental cultures from several locations had tested positive for anthrax, suggesting an even higher potential for contamination than previously thought. Decisions were made independently by the House and Senate leadership to close their respective office buildings to allow more comprehensive testing.

When the Senate leadership presented the decision to the full membership, though, they learned that senators felt strongly that their session on Thursday should go on as scheduled. During the meeting, I briefly addressed my colleagues, offering my views from a medical standpoint on the anthrax exposure so far. Our discussion seemed to reassure many of them.

After hearing from officials involved in the investigation, several senators made it clear that they believed Senate business should not be stopped, because it would be a sign of giving in to the terrorists. At the time, most felt that the events occurring on the Hill were likely related to the September 11 attacks. This was, many believed, round two of the assault on the nation's capital. A plane had struck the Pentagon and killed 189. Another that crashed in Pennsylvania, killing 44, almost certainly was headed for Washington. And now, many thought, came deadly anthrax, aimed at the highest-ranking member of the U.S. Senate.

In the end, we decided to close the Senate office buildings later that day but to stay in session in the Capitol building itself on Thursday. House members, in a separate meeting, decided to close their office buildings and to adjourn. The press made a big deal about the House leaving and the Senate staying. It was an uncomfortable situation for both houses, with accusations flying back and forth, mostly fueled by the press.

To me, this just reflected an initial miscommunication between the House and the Senate at the leadership level, in large part arising from the lack of certainty surrounding the interpretation of environmental culture results that were slowly coming back. Apparently, House and Senate leaders had left the earlier morning meeting with different understandings as to what they would do regarding closing the buildings. Policy decisions that could affect the safety of personnel had to be made on the basis of incomplete information and inadequate science. Such is the nature of bioterrorism.

At the request of the Senate leadership, I briefed the chiefs of staff of all the senators in the basement of the Capitol at 1 P.M. It was a tense meeting. The same officials who had briefed senators in the morning gave a quick update, but the high-level staffers in the room were angry, frustrated, and resentful. And appropriately (though unavoidably) so. They were responsible for their offices, they said, yet they were not getting any information to tell their staff members. Were they safe? Why were senators getting briefed early and the staffers so much later? Had they been exposed to something that could harm them? Were the clothes they were wearing safe, or could spores on the clothing be taken home and infect their children? When could they get back in their offices? How would they get their information if they were at home without access to their computers? Just listening and doing my best to respond made me realize how critical communication is, especially in times of terror.

With offices closing, the normal flow of information through e-mail was instantly cut off because people could no longer get to their office computers, and they couldn't access internal Senate information from their home computers. At the staff meeting, I announced that I would make my official personal Senate website available for the foreseeable future, posting all the information to which I had access. I gave them the website address (Frist .senate.gov) and instructed my staff to stay on it full-time to keep it current throughout the developing situation.

The website contained basic information about anthrax as well as particular ways to deal with this recent attack, including the protocol for opening mail, easy-to-access references, frequently asked questions, and updated information about the current test results, how to obtain your test results, and where additional individuals could be tested. It became a central repository for information for staffers and senators alike.

Everyone wanted to know more about skin and inhalational anthrax, and the initial TV news reports by political figures and health officials were confusing. What does the rash look like? Even as a physician familiar with infectious diseases because of my transplant experience, I'd never seen it. So I immediately called my colleagues around the country, found pictures of the rashes, and within a few hours posted them on the website for the world to see. As questions came throughout the next several days, we posted them with the best answers available. What about pregnant women who were exposed? Go to the website. What are the side effects of Cipro? Go the website. You could not get that information from the family doctor because the doctor had never been taught about the symptoms and signs of anthrax disease. The answers generally are not in medical textbooks because anthrax is too rare. But we were able to get it all up quickly on a centralized website. Another lesson learned.

Because of my long-standing interest in bioterrorism and the work I had done putting together the Public Health Threats and Emergencies Act of 2000 a year previously, I already had a section on bioterrorism on my site. I was able to expand it quickly over a few hours and updated it twice a day as reports came out of the public health command room at the Senate. My staff made sure this site was linked to other reputable sites with useful information on bioterrorism, biological agents, and public health safety, including the CDC (the overall best site) and other government and university sites. Thousands of people in Washington began to visit our site. Indeed, because it provided current and accurate information, people from around the country began to use it as a primary site.

Thankfully, other than the initial twenty-eight staffers, no one else on the Hill tested positive for exposure to anthrax. So only individuals on the fifth and sixth floors of the southeast corridor of the Hart building were initially given the sixty-day course of antibiotics. (All the nasal swab tests reported for my staff were negative, although one individual's test result was lost.)

More than six thousand nasal swabs were tested through the Capitol attending physician's office alone. In addition, thousands of environmental cultures were taken over the next several days. The laboratories were stretched to their limits, and their capacity to handle a sudden rush of new test requests—their "surge capacity"—was surpassed. People were working around the clock. When test results confirmed that anthrax contamination had been detected in the Dirksen Senate Office Building mailroom and elsewhere in the Hart building, as well as in one of the House buildings, the decision was made to close all of the congressional buildings Thursday until further environmental tests could be completed.

This only added to the anxiety of several thousand staffers who were left to wonder whether they had been exposed and were at risk for anthrax infection. Paralysis began to set in.

THURSDAY

We held two press conferences on Thursday, still operating with the same team of public health officials out of the command center on the third floor. The CDC continued to send new people up from Atlanta, but there was crucial consistency in leadership in the command center throughout this period.

Having two press conferences separated by only six hours allowed us to answer the onslaught of questions from the media and provide updates as we continued to glean new facts. But equally important, these press conferences gave all of us the opportunity to establish who the public health command team was and to explain to the public what anthrax is, what the relative risk of exposure is, what Cipro is and what its side effects are, how anthrax is treated, and what the difference is between nasal swabs that measure exposure and other tests that measure disease.

On Thursday, the testing site was moved out of the Senate office buildings off Capitol Hill to a day care center about three blocks away. Anxious to see if this new site, identified only late the night before, could be set up that quickly to handle the hundreds, and maybe thousands, of people requesting testing and antibiotics and information, I stopped by the off-site test facility early that morning. I was impressed. I especially respected the uniformed public health officials who took the swabs, counseled anxious people, and handed out antibiotics. I had the director of our health subcommittee staff go by the site every two hours to make sure that things ran smoothly over the course of the day.

The line initially wrapped around two sides of a city block. But all were calm, although most had to wait an hour in line, and things ran efficiently. The only hitch came when parents complained that we should not have allowed the name of the day care center to appear in the paper.

FRIDAY

By Friday, it seemed as if the anthrax outbreak had been contained. Everyone who had been exposed had been identified, and all were being treated. Based on everything we knew from both a scientific and a public policy standpoint, no one would get sick. All was under control.

Communication, though imperfect, had improved. The almost hourly thirst for new culture results and test results seemed to be subsiding since most tests had been completed. People had grown accustomed to the now familiar voices of those on the Hill, including me, who stepped up to the microphones to explain what was happening.

Yet, we were still operating in a new atmosphere characterized by much uncertainty. There was so much we didn't know. How will people respond to long-term use of antibiotics? Could we have missed someone? Was it possible someone had just been visiting the Hart building on Monday and then traveled back across the country, now unaware that he should be on antibiotics? Could the ventilation system have spread the spores farther than we thought? And what about the Dirksen mailroom? How could it have been contaminated?

Should we have paid more attention to that?

The answer, we soon learned, was yes. We should have.

SATURDAY

The calm was short-lived. On Saturday morning, I went to the Capitol to attend what I thought would be a short briefing among all of us on the response team and to plan additional steps for the upcoming week.

At the beginning of the meeting, someone at the table mentioned that the CDC team had been contacted by a local community physician Friday evening. A patient a few miles away from Capitol Hill had presented with signs and symptoms that might possibly be consistent with the inhalation form of anthrax: shortness of breath, an abnormal chest X ray with enlarged lymph nodes but clear lung fields. But the symptoms were also consistent with the flu. No blood cultures or other tests had confirmed the presence of anthrax, but all the pertinent tests were pending. The results would not be back for another twenty-four hours.

When I heard the details, I was startled—truly alarmed. I realized then that what I'd thought would continue to be a relatively controlled situation on Capitol Hill, with all potential victims already identified and appropriately treated, might abruptly become a national emergency.

According to everything we knew to be true about anthrax at the time, it would have been impossible for someone miles away from where the anthrax-laced envelope was opened to have been infected with the disease. We had relied on our current textbook understanding of the disease: Inhalational anthrax disease does not occur unless there is direct inhalation of more than ten thousand spores.

Given that numerous witnesses saw the letter opened in the suite of offices in the Hart building, it did not seem possible that enough spores could have escaped to infect someone who wasn't fairly close to where the letter was opened.

What we were discovering was that even the information from the best medical scientists and public health specialists in the United States was wrong. Dead wrong. We did not know enough. No one did. We as a nation were underprepared scientifically for bioterrorism.

Although the test results would not be back for another day and the clinical data were really not very clear, I believed the information could portend a national catastrophe. Was this part of a much bigger conspiracy or terrorist activity? Would we start seeing cases around the country now? Were postal workers safe? Would our mail system be shut down locally—or possibly nationally—just as the air transportation system had been paralyzed a month previously by the terrorist attacks on Washington and New York?

What was next?

With bioterrorism, the perpetrator doesn't have to be present, the weapon is invisible, and the victims may not become apparent until days after exposure. It is much different from any other type of crime.

The one thing I knew was that all certainty had disappeared. We were seeing things happen that had never even been envisioned by scientific or health officials. Just as five weeks before, the September 11 terrorist attacks at the Pentagon and World Trade Centers were beyond what anyone had ever envisioned could happen.

I immediately got up, went across the room to the telephone, and called the White House. I asked to speak to Tom Ridge. Just a few weeks earlier, Ridge, the former governor of Pennsylvania, had been appointed homeland security director by President Bush. Governor Ridge called back immediately, and I told him that we no longer had a local public health situation but a potential national emergency, with disease appearing and behaving like we had never seen before. I said that this could explode as a national security issue and a national public health emergency.

If people could get infected by simple exposure to mail (not the opening of mail), would we see others presenting with symptoms around the country over the next several days? Would we be prepared if they did? I asked Governor Ridge to give us a bit more time to get more information, and we agreed to have a conference call one hour later with the nation's highest officials in charge of emergency preparedness and response.

Within an hour, the team at our public health command center in the Capitol had a conference call with key figures from around the country: Tommy Thompson, secretary of health and human services; Bill Knous, director of the Health and Human Services Office of Emergency Preparedness; Dr. David Fleming, from the

CDC in Atlanta; Tom Ridge; and Joe Allbaugh, from the Federal Emergency Management Administration.

I opened the conference call and asked each of the members of the command team in the Capitol meeting room to speak for approximately five minutes. The goal was to share all that we had learned over the previous week on Capitol Hill with the federal officials on the conference call, who clearly would soon need to become more involved in the surveillance and response.

It was clearly stated that significantly more federal resources would be necessary to handle the increasing burdens placed by more extensive environmental testing and decontamination. The officials heard how the thousands of swab tests performed to date had stretched beyond the surge capacity of our public health system.

At the end of the conference call, I was certain that everyone on the phone understood the potential importance of the critical new suggestion that someone outside the immediate system had been infected. And they had a clear picture that our local resources had to be reinforced immediately with federal resources. In responding to bioterrorism, this vertical communication from local authorities directly to federal officials is vital.

Secretary Thompson closed the call, telling us to make a list of everything we would need. He assured us that it would be provided.

SUNDAY

Sunday morning at about ten o'clock, just before I was to go on one of the Sunday talk shows to discuss the developments on the Hill, I learned that the patient's test results had come back. The diagnosis was inhalational anthrax. The patient, we learned, worked at the Brentwood post office in Washington,D.C. Immediately, the local public health office, which had fortunately been a part of the public health command team from day one, fully mobilized and within hours began testing employees from the postal facility at a site made available by Washington's mayor, Anthony Williams.

That afternoon, I dropped by the District of Columbia office building where the testing was conducted. Again, it was impressive seeing groups of about twenty people at a time being moved from station to station, receiving information, counseling, testing, and antibiotics. The mood overall was pretty good. There was order. No panic. No anger.

Then again, no one had died—yet. But even as the testing was going on, another postal worker had entered the hospital, apparently with anthrax. Within two days, postal worker Thomas Morris Jr., fifty-five, had died. Later, a second postal worker, Joseph Curseen Jr., forty-seven, passed away.

These were tragic deaths that no one could have foreseen, knowing what we did at the time. We were basing all of our actions on specific clinical assumptions, the best information that could be found in the most current textbooks and medical literature, about a bacterium that we had been studying for centuries. We knew all of the identifying clinical features of anthrax—swelling of the lymph nodes of the middle of the chest and flulike symptoms—but our epidemiological understanding—our understanding of how the disease spreads—was inadequate.

And no one had realized it.

Our assumptions had been based principally on how the anthrax bacterium acted in settings that were almost preindustrial—before most buildings were air conditioned, before technology allowed us to sort mail with the force of air, and before we had advanced medical technologies to help us stabilize patients and make more definitive diagnoses. For the most part, what we knew about anthrax was based on how it occurred naturally—not on how it could be used by terrorists with the intent to kill and to terrorize. These are new times.

We had to reexamine our assumptions about anthrax—about the likelihood of contracting inhalational anthrax compared to cutaneous anthrax, about the relative risk to those who had little or no contact with the actual anthrax-laced letter, and about the best ways to diagnose and treat those with the disease.

As with all areas of medicine, the body of knowledge is an ever changing enterprise, updated daily with more information from various studies. However, we had not updated our understanding of anthrax or other potential biological agents in years, primarily because of a lack of data.

In short, we weren't ready for what occurred.

Once the impact of anthrax spread beyond Capitol Hill and into the U.S. postal system, spokespersons for this national issue were the federal officials charged with responding to this threat. I continued answering questions on television shows and the news, providing information about our response to this particular biological attack as well as to any future attacks.

Given that my website received as many as forty thousand hits a day, it was clear that people were hungry for knowledge. Generally, as I have discussed bioterrorism in recent months, people ask many of the same questions. I've noticed that when people get timely, straightforward answers to their questions, they become more relaxed and reassured. And that's why I am writing this book—to answer the questions most frequently asked, to discuss some of the questions you may have thought about but never asked, to help reassure and inform American families about bioterrorism.

The purpose is to provide information that's as reliable and accurate as possible, to as many people as possible, in these times of greater-than-normal anxiety. Our nation is on high alert. We're being faced with new challenges, in our places of work and in our homes. But our nation, our officials at all levels of government, and the American people are taking the steps necessary now to be prepared to meet whatever challenge comes our way.

Toward this end there are things that each and every one of us can do. One of the most powerful is to become knowledgeable and informed. An understanding of some of the basics on how to prepare for, and respond to, the use of microbes as weapons goes a long way to reduce anxiety and minimize any chance of paralysis in our lives.

In the war against bioterrorism, information is power.

2

SAFE AT HOME
A Family Survival Guide

Americans have suddenly had to come face-to-face with the now very real threat of the use of biological and chemical agents against them and their loved ones. The risk is small, tiny in fact. But there is risk, and unfortunately, as recent times have so vividly illustrated, it is increasing.

Everywhere I've gone in recent months, people have asked me what they can do to protect themselves and their loved ones from the threat of bioterrorism. They want to know how to cope effectively with the stress and anxiety it can cause.

Our family has been affected by the events of last fall. Every family has. My wife, Karyn, and I have three boys: Bryan, who is fourteen years old; Jonathan, sixteen; and Harrison, eighteen. They watched me live through the frightening uncertainty of the anthrax exposure on Capitol Hill, and I've done my best to address their concerns about the events surrounding September 11 and the anthrax-laced letter that was mailed to my colleague Senator Daschle.

At their school events, I receive many questions from concerned parents regarding what they should tell their children and how they can help them live without fear. My purpose here is to answer as many of those questions as I can, as specifically and practically as I can.

In this chapter, I won't deal with the government's preparation and response. I'll cover that thoroughly in the final chapter. In the chapters that follow, I'll answer the pertinent questions about the main, specific bioterrorism threats that we face, such as anthrax and smallpox.

Here, our focus is simply on what families need to know and do to be as prepared as they can be for this threat our nation faces. Just to be clear, there is a huge difference between being prepared and living in fear. One of the most perceptive things I read in the aftermath of the anthrax attacks last fall was written by columnist Jonathan Alter in *Newsweek*. Recounting his experiences working in the New York offices of NBC when an anthrax-tainted letter was delivered there, Alter wrote, "Anthrax is not contagious, but fear is."

Precisely. There is no reason for paralysis in our everyday lives, and clearly no cause for panic. But there is good reason for every American, young and old, to know much more about what in these times might confront them. *Bio*terrorism personalizes terror like no other type of terrorism. But there are steps each of us can take to reduce our vulnerabilities and thereby restore our sense of security and safety.

WHAT IS BIOTERRORISM?

Bioterrorism is the intentional release of potentially deadly bacteria, viruses, or toxins into the air, food, or water supply.

Ounce for ounce, biological agents such as anthrax and smallpox are among the most lethal weapons of mass destruction known. Inhalation of a millionth of a gram of anthrax may be deadly. In

1993, the Office of Technology Assessment estimated that under certain atmospheric conditions dispersion by airplane of 220 pounds of anthrax spores over Washington, D.C., could result in up to three million deaths.

That's a worst-case scenario. But even on a much smaller scale, a bioterrorist attack could be designed to instill fear in our people.

"As I see it, the goal of bioterrorism is not as much to do mortal harm as it is to disrupt our way of life and make us clearly aware of our vulnerability," says Larry Bush, M.D., infectious disease specialist at the John F. Kennedy Medical Center in Atlantis, Florida. "Though recent events have proven this successful, we will now be both intellectually and emotionally better prepared."

Bioterrorism is certainly not a new phenomenon. Biological weapons are as old as mankind, going back to Hannibal, who won a naval battle in 190 B.C. by firing earthen vessels full of poisonous snakes into his enemy's flagship. Recent use of bioweapons has only exposed and affirmed our nation's and other countries' vulnerability to these agents.

The mailing of anthrax-laced letters to U.S. Senate offices and media outlets last fall infected eighteen people and killed five. Tens of thousands more who were exposed to the potentially lethal biological agent were initially treated with antibiotics, and even though the attacks were confined to the East Coast, the impact could be felt across our land.

But this wasn't the first time our nation was subjected to bioterrorism. In rural Oregon in the 1980s, members of a religious commune, in a plot to make large segments of the population too sick to vote, sprinkled salmonella on the salad bars of several restaurants in the county. Over 750 people became ill.

And in 1995 the Aum Shinrikyo "Supreme Truth" cult staged an attack with the chemical agent Sarin in the Tokyo subway system. The attack killed twelve people and injured five thousand. The cult also was working with bioweapons, including anthrax and botulinum toxin.

CAN WE EXPECT MORE BIOTERROR EVENTS IN THE WAKE OF THE ANTHRAX-LETTER ATTACK?

It is no longer a question of if but when and where and how.

Just as many of us never imagined that American commercial airliners would be converted into weapons of mass destruction, it is perhaps beyond the grasp of many that the weapons of choice in the first war of the twenty-first century may be tularemia, smallpox, and anthrax. But this should come as no surprise.

The threats from biological and chemical agents are real. Terrorist groups have the resources and the motivation to use germ warfare. Well before the September 11 attacks, Osama bin Laden publicly stated that it was his religious duty to acquire weapons of mass destruction, including biological and chemical weapons. And when our troops went through hideouts abandoned by bin Laden's terrorist network, al Qaeda, they reportedly found evidence of efforts to develop biological and chemical weapons.

For years, we assumed that no nation or group—even terrorists—would use biological weapons because of the universal condemnation their use would surely bring from all corners of the world. Sadly, we know better now.

If anything, bioterrorism is likely to be embraced by terrorist organizations for several reasons. As we have seen, they often are driven by fanatical religious beliefs and deep-rooted ethnic struggles. There clearly is no limit to the level of violence and death they find acceptable in support of their twisted goals.

In addition, rapid advances in the technology needed to deliver biological agents have made the weaponization of germs much easier. And, with the fall of the Soviet Union, the expertise of thousands of scientists knowledgeable in germ warfare may be available to the highest bidder.

There are other advantages for terrorists in using a biological agent over other methods of attack. It is very difficult to trace a bioagent back to its source. In general, neither sophisticated knowledge nor significant resources are required to launch a bioterrorist attack, and the materials are relatively easy to acquire. It has been estimated that a substantial biological arsenal could be developed in a fifteen-foot-square room with just $10,000 of equipment.

Biological weapons pose considerable security challenges that are different from those of standard terrorist devices. They are not detected by methods used for explosives and firearms, such as metal detectors and x-ray devices. They are invisible. The first indication of an attack is the development of symptoms by those exposed. Yet, victims of a covert bioterrorist attack do not necessarily develop symptoms immediately upon exposure to the bioagent. Symptoms may occur days later, long after the bioweapon is dispersed.

As a result, people who are exposed will most likely arrive in emergency rooms, physician offices, and urgent-care centers or clinics with symptoms that mimic the common cold or flu. In all likelihood, physicians and other health care providers will not attribute these symptoms to a bioweapon. If the bioagent is communicable, such as smallpox, many more people—including health care workers—may be infected before doctors know what they're dealing with.

WHEN THE NATION IS PUT ON "HIGH ALERT," WHAT SPECIFIC ACTIONS SHOULD I TAKE?

After the September 11 attacks, the federal government issued several notices placing law enforcement agencies and the military on "high alert" when credible information of possible terrorist attacks had been compiled by intelligence sources. At the same time, general alerts were issued to the public.

The alerts are a way for the federal government to let citizens know that the military and law enforcement agencies are increasing their vigilance and that citizens should, too. I know people feel frustrated because they don't know exactly what to do. It can be stressful for them and their families.

Frankly, our government is in a tough spot on this one. If we receive what we believe is credible information regarding a possible terrorist attack—even if key details such as when and where are missing—shouldn't the government let the people know? President Bush believes we should, and I agree.

But is there really anything you can do to help? Absolutely. First and foremost, you can be the eyes and ears of our law enforcement agencies. You know your communities better than anyone else. You know when something looks out of place, whether it's a package left on the subway or someone acting in an unusual or suspicious manner in your neighborhood.

Being more vigilant empowers you to be part of our war to rid the world of the evil of terrorism. Be more conscious of what's going on around you. Report any suspicious activity or behavior to local authorities. But vigilance alone is not enough. You should take additional steps now to plan and prepare for how your family will respond if there is a bioterrorist or some other form of attack.

WHEN I'M IN PUBLIC, WHAT SHOULD I LOOK FOR?

Terrorists tend to choose highly visible targets where large numbers of people gather. These would include large cities, international airports, subway systems, resorts, historic landmarks, and major sporting and entertainment events.

It's not that people should avoid these places. In fact, it's important that we not give in to fear by allowing the terrorists to change the way we live. Instead, whenever you're in one of these situations, just be a little more aware of your surroundings.

Learn where the emergency exits and staircases are. Plan ahead how you would get out quickly in an emergency.

If you're traveling, take note of any conspicuous or unusual behavior. Don't accept packages from strangers, and never leave your luggage unattended.

WHAT SHOULD I DO IF I FIND MYSELF IN THE MIDDLE OF A SCENE THAT MIGHT INVOLVE BIOLOGICAL OR CHEMICAL MATERIALS?

Don't panic! Yes, every situation is different, but there are general steps that will minimize risk to you and your loved ones. And these apply to both biological and chemical events.

1. If you're outside, evaluate the suspected area from a position upwind, cover all exposed skin surfaces, and protect your respiratory system as much as possible, perhaps using a handkerchief to cover your mouth and nose.

2. If the incident is inside, leave immediately and try to avoid the contaminated area on your way out. Keep windows and unused doors closed. Turn off the ventilation system (air-conditioning or heat). If you are inside and the event is outside, stay inside. Turn off the ventilation system and seal windows and doors with plastic tape.

3. Call 911 and report the following:
   ❑ Your name and phone number
   ❑ Date and time of event
   ❑ Distance from the incident or point of impact
   ❑ Reason for the report (for example, people becoming sick, a vapor cloud, dead or sick animals or birds, unusual odors, dead or discolored vegetation)
   ❑ Location of the incident
   ❑ Description of the terrain (for example, flat, hills, river)

❏ Weather

❏ Temperature

❏ Odor (for example, none, sweet, fruity, pepper, garlic, rotten eggs)

❏ Visible emission (for example, none, smoke, haze)

❏ Symptoms (for example, none, dizziness, runny nose, choking, tightness in chest, blurred vision, fever, difficulty breathing, stinging of skin, welts/blisters, headaches, nausea, and vomiting) and time they appeared

❏ Explosion (for example, none, air, ground, structure, underground) and location

4. Once clear of the suspected contaminated area, remove all external clothing and leave it outside. Proceed directly (within minutes) to a shower and thoroughly wash with soap and water, scrubbing aggressively to cover every part of your body with at least ten scrubbing motions. Irrigate your eyes with water.

WHAT KIND OF PLAN DO I NEED FOR MY FAMILY?

Every family should have a disaster plan. If yours doesn't, start discussing a plan tonight at the dinner table. Even without the threat of bioterrorism, this is a sound idea. The current world situation only reinforces the need for preparedness. We're not talking about bomb shelters here or the pre-Y2K hysteria to which some fell prey. The things you should do to safeguard your family in case of a bioterrorist attack are basically the same as what you would do for any natural disaster.

Your plan should cover three essential elements, according to the American Red Cross:

• Communication: How will you communicate with family

members if there is a bioterrorist attack or some other disaster?

- Destination: Where will your family go if there is an attack?

- Supplies: What supplies should you have on hand in case you need to "shelter at home" for a while?

WHAT KIND OF COMMUNICATIONS PLAN DO I NEED?

Choose one person who lives out of state to be your family's contact in case of emergency. Why? In a disaster, it's often easier to call long distance than to make a local call. Everyone in your family should know the phone number.

Also, choose a family meeting place outside your neighborhood in case you can't go home. Again, everyone in your family should know the address and phone number.

In addition, you should have a backup out-of-state contact and a backup meeting place, just for insurance. And be sure to discuss your plan routinely with family members so that it becomes second nature. That will help prevent panic if disaster does strike.

WHERE SHOULD MY FAMILY GO IF THERE'S A BIOTERRORIST ATTACK?

That obviously will depend on how close the attack occurs to your home. The most likely scenario appears to be that emergency officials would urge people to shelter at home in the event of a bioterrorist attack. So designate a "safe room" in your home, one with a telephone and radio. Choose an interior room without windows, if possible. Don't use the basement, however, because—in a chemical attack—heavier chemical vapors would tend to sink to the lowest place in a house. Gather your family in the safe room and listen to the news for further instructions.

If officials order an evacuation, make sure everyone in your family knows in advance how to get outside from every room in the house. Where possible, devise two escape routes from every room, in case one is blocked.

WHAT ABOUT DISASTER SUPPLY KITS? WHAT SUPPLIES SHOULD I HAVE IN CASE OF A BIOTERROR ATTACK?

Disaster supply kits are just what they imply: a collection of basic supplies that are readily available in the event there is a "worst-case scenario" that requires you and your family to become fully self-sufficient for several days. In the case of bioterrorism, this might occur because stores are closed and other social services interrupted. The disaster kit for bioterrorism is not very different from that required for other types of emergencies.

Pack essential supplies in an easy-to-carry container such as a large, covered trash can, a duffel bag, or a camping backpack. Store this disaster supply kit where it can be easily reached, and make sure every family member knows where it is. That way, you can grab it quickly whether you have to remain inside or evacuate.

Your disaster supply kit should include the following items:

❑ Water. Store in plastic containers such as large soft-drink bottles. Have at least a three-day supply, figuring on one gallon a day for each person. Change the water in your kit at least every six months.

❑ Canned food. At least a three-day supply. Good items include canned meats, fruits, and vegetables; juices,

milk, and soups; high-energy snacks such as peanut
butter, jelly, crackers, "power bars," and trail mix;
candy and cookies; instant coffee and tea bags; and any
special foods for infants, the elderly, or those on special
diets. Avoid salty items, though, as they will make you
drink more water. Write the date on the food items and
change foods at least every six months. Be sure to
check expiration dates on labels. An easy way to
remember to update your water and food supplies is to
change items at the beginning and end of daylight sav-
ings time, when you also change the batteries in smoke
detectors.

❏ Nonelectric can opener.
❏ Cell phone.
❏ Change of clothing. One extra set of clothes and
footwear for each member of the family.
❏ Goggles. One pair for each member of the family, to pro-
tect the eyes. Swimmer's goggles are fine.
❏ Respirators for each family member. These are filtered
fiber masks and only cost about $1 each. Look for ones
with N95 certification. (I'll explain what that means in
just a bit.)
❏ Roll of plastic tape, such as package-sealing tape (to seal
windows, if necessary).
❏ Flashlight with extra batteries.
❏ Portable radio with extra batteries.
❏ Portable heater.
❏ Thermal blankets or sleeping bags. One for each mem-
ber of the family.
❏ Extra car keys, credit card, and cash.
❏ Extra pair of eyeglasses.
❏ Special items for infants or elderly or disabled family
members.

❑   First aid kit, including:
    — A ten-day supply of your family's prescription med-
      ications
    — Painkillers, such as ibuprofen, acetaminophen, or
      aspirin
    — Antihistamines, if family members have allergies
    — Mild laxative
    — Antidiarrhea medication, such as Pepto-Bismol,
      Kaopectate, or Imodium AD

If you have pets, include the following items in your supply kit:

❑   Identification collar and rabies tag
❑   Carrier or cage
❑   Leash
❑   Medications
❑   Newspapers, litter, trash bags for waste
❑   Two-week supply of food and water
❑   Veterinary records (necessary if your pet has to go to a
    shelter)

THERE ARE ALL KINDS OF DIFFERENT MASKS ON THE MARKET. WHICH OFFERS THE BEST PROTECTION FOR MY FAMILY?

The best bet, I believe, is a simple mask with a filter that covers
your mouth and nose and can block extremely tiny particles. The
technical term for this kind of mask, manufactured by 3M as well
as other companies, is a "respirator." Look for one with the rating
of N95. I'll explain what that means in a minute.

There are generally three categories of masks: ones that enclose
the entire head ("full-face"), ones that cover the mouth and nose
("half-face"), and the simple disposable masks where the mask
itself serves as a filter.

If fitted correctly—and this is harder than it sounds—respirators can reduce exposure to anthrax bacteria and other harmful agents. It is very difficult, however, to achieve a perfect fit with these simple masks. It takes about fifteen minutes to adjust the mask to fit your face the right way. So just owning one, without a proper fitting, may provide a false sense of security.

Now, about the rating. Filters are tested by the National Institute for Occupational Safety and Health (NIOSH). The rating reflects how efficiently the filter blocks tiny microscopic test particles of 0.3 microns in diameter. A filter with a 95 rating filters out at least 95 percent of the particles in a test. A filter with a 100 rating filters out 99.7 percent of the particles.

Filters are also classified into one of three categories: N, P, or R. N means the filter was tested with sodium chloride particles. P signifies that the filter is impenetrable by oils. R signifies that a filter is *resistant* to oils.

So you need to understand that N95 masks only *reduce* exposure to particles, they don't eliminate it entirely. Since at this point we still don't know exactly how many anthrax spores, for example, it takes to infect a person, there's no guarantee that wearing a mask would offer complete protection—even if it screens out 95 percent of the particles.

The majority of filters you'll hear about are N95, P100, or N100. All N95 through P100 masks should be fit tested. The Occupational Safety and Health Administration (OSHA) does not require fit testing for disposable N95 masks if they are worn voluntarily. You should be aware that any facial hair where the mask meets the skin greatly reduces the efficiency of the mask.

A more expensive option is the rubbery half-face mask that has filters protruding on the sides. It's called an "elastomeric respirator," in industry terms. Elastomeric masks have replaceable filters that screw on and off, and the synthetic material of the mask can be disinfected with cleaning material. The P100 elastomeric mask does the best job of protecting against biological agents.

HOW MUCH DO THESE MASKS COST, AND WHERE DO I GET THEM?

Prices for masks vary. Disposable N95 respirators are about $1 each. N100 disposables are around $5. Disposable respirators are available at most hardware or paint stores.

Available at hardware or industrial-supply stores, elastomeric masks are about $20 each, and filters can be purchased for $5 and up, depending on the efficiency of the filter. All NIOSH-approved filters are marked as such on the box, the filter itself, or in the instructions—look for the NIOSH approval.

The less expensive but widely marketed "dust and nuisance" masks are not NIOSH approved and are essentially ineffective for biological agents. But they are useful for visible dust.

The top respirator manufacturers are 3M, Moldex, and MSA.

ARE THESE FILTERED MASKS USEFUL FOR CHEMICAL AGENTS AS WELL?

None of the industrial masks mentioned above are effective against chemical agents. Chemicals are effectively filtered by using acti-vated-carbon filters that are treated with impregnate. Different filters are typically made for specific chemicals. However, some manufacturers make carbon filters that protect against several different chemicals.

Military-type gas masks that protect against chemicals are not rated by NIOSH for use because they physically restrict breathing and could harm the general public. Highly sophisticated "supplied-air" respirators that deliver their own self-contained clean air are effective for most chemical exposures. However, no respirator is capable of preventing all airborne contaminants from entering the wearer's breathing zone. A mask is ineffective against contaminants that can penetrate exposed skin, such as sulfur mustard gas.

Within a year, NIOSH and the U.S. Department of Defense will for the first time come up with specific approval standards for protection against chemical and biological weapons.

DO SIMPLE FIBER MASKS OFFER PROTECTION AGAINST BIOLOGICAL AND CHEMICAL AGENTS?

Fiber masks without filters are simple masks that cover the mouth and nose, similar to those you see surgeons wearing on television. The main purpose of these simple masks is to keep out dust and other particles that may fill the air in disasters such as the World Trade Center attack. Fiber masks without filters will not be very useful in a biological or chemical attack because the mesh of fiber masks is not small enough to keep out the very tiny biological or chemical agents. Only gas masks and other specialized industrial masks will work in such situations, and even they would have to be worn at the time of the attack. Putting a mask on after you were exposed would be too late.

Therefore, I recommend that you include in your disaster supply kit an N95 NIOSH-rated mask for each of your family members. Without a personalized fitting, however, this mask offers only limited protection against biological agents—better than a simple fiber non-filtered mask, but not as complete as industrial-grade respirators.

SHOULD I BUY A "GAS MASK?"

The interest in gas masks when faced with the threat of biological or chemical attack is certainly understandable, especially when you learn that so many of the biological agents are so deadly when they are inhaled into the lungs.

True industrial-grade gas masks can protect against biological as well as chemical agents. A sophisticated, powered, air-purifying respirator with high-efficiency particulate air (HEPA) filters, when properly fitted, can reduce inhalation exposures by 98 percent.

But—and this is a very important point—this kind of mask is effective *only* if you are wearing it at the time of the attack.

If there is a biological or chemical attack, one thing is virtually certain: It will come without warning. And that's really the key issue here, in terms of the practical question about buying a gas mask. Unless you have enough advance warning to get the mask, put the right filter in, and make sure it's fitted properly, it won't do you any good.

And the odds of that happening are slim. In an urban setting such as New York, sheltering in your safe room and immediately turning off the ventilation system (heat or air conditioner) is likely to be more useful than a gas mask.

HOW CAN I DECONTAMINATE AN AREA SUSPECTED OF BEING HIT BY A BIOLOGICAL OR CHEMICAL ATTACK?

Although your natural reaction might be to immediately decontaminate an area, check with your local public health authority first, because you may be putting yourself at risk by further exposure to the offending agent during the cleanup. Moreover, you may lose important information and evidence that could be useful to a law enforcement investigation.

For suspected biological and chemical decontamination, the contaminated areas can be washed with a 0.5 percent sodium hypochlorite solution, allowing a contact time of ten to fifteen minutes. To make a 0.5 percent sodium hypochlorite solution, take one part household bleach, such as Clorox, and ten parts water. Keep this solution away from your eyes.

If biological or chemical contamination is suspected on fabric, clothing, or equipment, you can decontaminate with undiluted household bleach. Leave it on for thirty minutes before discarding or using the item.

THE SEPTEMBER 11 ATTACK WAS THE MOST TERRIFYING EVENT OF MY LIFE. HOW CAN I DEAL WITH THE STRESS AND ANXIETY I FEEL LIVING ON HIGH ALERT?

First, realize that you're not alone! A nationwide study showed that nine out of ten Americans showed some clinical sign of stress the week after the September 11 terrorist attacks. And almost half of all adults reported at least one substantial symptom of stress, such as having difficulty sleeping or uncalled-for outbursts of anger.

We can learn much from others around the world. Citizens in Israel and Northern Ireland have been living under the threat of terrorism for years. They have experienced the terror but have accommodated and adapted and been able to regain normalcy in their lives.

We know from research that while the effects of a disaster such as the terrorist attacks typically lessen with time, they can linger for years and may resurface from time to time.

So what are the signs that you're continuing to feel stress over the terrorist threat?

Reactions may be physical or emotional. Among the physical symptoms are backaches, headaches, stomachaches, diarrhea, nausea, and shortness of breath.

Emotional symptoms include shock, disbelief, fear, grief, anxiety, disorientation, hyperalertness, being easily startled, nightmares, crying, anger, irritability, detachment, numbness, feelings of betrayal, survivor guilt, isolation, depression, inability to concentrate or carry on normal activities, a sense of loss of control, revival of past traumatic memories, apathy, and decreased ability to feel joy.

If you're experiencing any of these signs, know two things: You're not alone. And there are simple steps you can take to feel better. Here's what mental health experts recommend to relieve stress and anxiety:

- *Talk with others.* This is a time to draw closer to those you love and trust, not push them away. And chances are they're feeling many of the same things as you. Just giving voice to what you're feeling inside can lessen stress.

- *Keep the faith.* For many of us, faith was a source of comfort and strength in the wake of the unspeakable horror we witnessed. As a medical doctor, I know the healing power of prayer. In these difficult times, prayer can help ease anxiety and bring us together. This is a time to draw strength from the traditions of your church, synagogue, mosque, or temple. Knowing that God is just and that he is in control offers great comfort when we feel so powerless.

- *Embrace your daily routines.* It's important for all of us to go about our lives as normally as possible. If you're feeling like your life is spinning out of control, the simple, productive daily routines—whether it's taking a walk, listening to an audio book on your commute to work, or shuttling the kids to soccer practice and music lessons—offer calming reassurance that life does go on. In particular, make a point of doing the things you do well. Whether it's baking cookies, playing basketball with your daughter, doing a crossword puzzle, crocheting a scarf—whatever, it doesn't matter. The idea is to feel once again that sense of being in control and excelling at something.

- *Take a news break.* Television news can become seductive.

It's important for all of us to be informed. But with twenty-four-hour cable news networks, the Internet, and a huge assortment of newspapers and newsmagazines, it's easy to feel overwhelmed by too much information. And this can heighten your anxiety. In the week after the September 11 attacks, adults and children watched on average an hour more of television a day, and those who watched the most TV news coverage exhibited the most signs of stress. Again, this isn't to say that watching the news, reading the newspaper, listening to the radio, or checking out your favorite news sites on the Web is harmful in any way. It's a matter of being selective about how much news you get. If your news habits are feeding your anxiety, it's time to cut back.

- *Show your colors.* We saw a rebirth of overt, good old-fashioned patriotism after September 11. And that is a magnificent and healthy reaction. The greatest thing about the American people is our indomitable spirit. The outpouring of generosity and caring this country witnessed after the September 11 attacks made me so proud of this nation that I love. Seeing yourself as part of this great land is more important now than ever before. If you're feeling isolated or not in control, small acts can help. Wear a flag lapel pin. Our family put up a large permanent flagpole in our yard so we could fly the American flag daily. Send a donation to a local charity. Get involved in your community's preparedness plan. Do what you can to support your country during these trying times.

- *Join a group.* A sense of community, of belonging to something larger than yourself, goes a long way in overcoming feelings of isolation. Shared interests can help you expand your network of friends. So join a book group, take a modern dance class, sign up to study a foreign language—again, whatever interests you, whatever you've always wanted to do.

One of the encouraging signs from the nationwide study on post–September 11 stress is how many Americans turned to these coping strategies to deal with the anxiety they felt. According to the study, which was done by the Rand Corporation and the University of California at Los Angeles, 98 percent of those responding to the survey said they talked with others to help themselves cope; 90 percent said they turned to religion; 60 percent said they participated in group activities; and 36 percent said they made donations to relief funds.

Also, make sure you take proper care of yourself. Here are some other ways that mental health experts say you can relieve stress and anxiety:

- *Exercise regularly.* During stressful times, exercise often is the first thing to go. You may not feel like you have the time or energy to exercise. But that's precisely when you need it the most. Exercise can actually boost your energy and give you a greater sense of control. Going to the gym is terrific, but there are lots of other ways to fit exercise into your hectic life. Start small. Walk with a coworker, friend, or family member at lunchtime. Take family hikes or bike rides on weekends. The key is to make exercise part of your routine. Just avoid exercising within three hours of bedtime, so it doesn't interfere with needed sleep.

- *Eat well.* Healthy eating is another of the first things to go during stressful times, usually for the same basic reasons as exercise: lack of time and energy. But just like exercise, eating regular meals with healthful foods is a great stress buster. Make sure you eat five to nine servings of fruits and vegetables daily, and avoid too much caffeine, sugar, and alcohol.

* *Get a good night's rest.* Tempting as it might be, turning to alcohol or relying too much on prescription or over-the-counter sleep aids can have a negative effect on your ability to get restful sleep. If you are having trouble sleeping, eliminate caffeine from your diet, talk or write about your concerns and worries before you try to sleep, and avoid late-night news or other activities that get you agitated. Take a warm bath. And, yes, drinking warm milk does help some people sleep.

One last note: Everyone copes with tragedy in different ways. There is no one right way. So be willing to experiment and find out what works for you. Recognize that it may take time before the stress and anxiety you feel subside. That's perfectly normal.

How long will I feel this way?

People are often surprised that reactions to trauma last longer than they expect. Resilient as we are, it may take weeks, months, or, in some cases, years to regain equilibrium. Traumatic experiences often remain vivid forever. Most of us will always be able to say where we were when we first learned of the terrorist attacks and the events that followed.

Some people will work things out with the help and support of family, friends, and colleagues. But these days, many are finding that they or their children have a number of stress reactions that won't go away or that interfere with work, school, home life, or leisure activities. Talking to a mental health trauma specialist can help. The key is to reach out—ask for help, support, understanding, and opportunities to talk.

ARE CHILDREN AT GREATER RISK FOR CERTAIN TYPES OF BIOTERRORISM THAN ADULTS?

They may be, and this is an area to which we need to devote a lot more research. Certainly for chemical weapons, this is true. Nerve agents, including Sarin—which I discuss in chapter 9—are denser than water, so they concentrate closer to the ground, in the breathing zone of a child.

Children breathe faster than adults, which would potentially place them at greater risk for inhalational agents. They are more likely to have minor cuts and scrapes, which could make it easier for germs to enter the body. For their body weight, children have a greater skin surface than adults, which could expose them more to blister agents, such as mustard gas. In addition, many of the potential bioterror agents cause vomiting and diarrhea, which can quickly lead to dehydration and shock in children.

To further complicate matters, the vaccines and antibiotics to fight these biological agents have generally not been studied as well in children as they have been in adults. The anthrax vaccine, for instance, has never been licensed for persons under eighteen.

But we in government are working to change this. Age-related research is critical. As new antibiotics and vaccines are approved, we must make sure that dosages and side effects are carefully studied in children as well as adults. As we work to improve our public health system's ability to respond to bioterrorism, we must do a better job of addressing the specific needs of children and make sure they're fully accounted for in all local and state planning as well as in the research for appropriate treatments.

How can we better prepare our children to cope with a major attack without making them afraid?

This is probably the question I've heard most from parents in recent months. We all want to do whatever we can to make sure our children are safe. But we certainly don't want them to have to live in constant fear. So how do we allow our children to lead normal, happy lives while being aware of, and prepared for, potential bioterrorist threats? That's a tough question. But it can be done.

A lot of the specific answers depend on the age of the child, and I'll deal with those differences in just a bit. But there are certain things that apply to all children.

First and foremost, spend more time with your children. Reassure them that you love them and will do everything in your power to keep them safe. You can't just think it. You've got to verbalize it and express it openly. How you do this will depend on how old your child is, although hugs and kisses are universally understood, from toddlers to teenagers.

Remember, like it or not, they'll take their cue from you. We all know that children are a lot more perceptive than we often give them credit for. They will pick up on any fear and anxiety you feel. So be mindful of what you say and do in front of your children.

If you're feeling overwhelmed by anxiety, anger, or grief, that's probably not the best time to talk with your children. But there's no reason to try to hide it, either. Just tell them right up front that you are feeling upset right now, so it's not a good time to talk. Let them know that you do want to talk to them, though, and that you will in a while, once you feel calmer. This lets children know that these feelings, as overwhelming as they may seem at the time, will pass and that adults can handle them. That can be very reassuring.

Just make sure that you really do talk with them later. It's important that parents don't become so wrapped up in their own feelings that they ignore their children's needs.

Also, regardless of how old your children are, listen before you talk. The only way you'll know what's really bothering your children is to let them tell you. Resist the temptation to lecture or tell them everything you think they need to know. Ask them what they've heard from friends, teachers, on the TV, or on the Internet.

Ask them what questions *they* have, and answer them as best you can in a direct and straightforward manner, with limited detail. Too much information can be overwhelming, especially for younger children. Often, they'll have only a couple of simple questions. That's fine.

Just keep in mind that your children may not always tell you in so many words that they're scared or worried. Those feelings may come through in their expressions, the way they play, or even by angry outbursts. Watch for dramatic changes in your children's behavior or mood, and if those changes persist, consider seeing a mental health professional.

One other thing to keep an eye on is your children's TV-viewing habits. Now, given the quality of television programming these days, that's good advice anyway for parents. But it's especially true when the airwaves are filled with around-the-clock news of terrorism or war.

If the news is on, watch it with them so you can talk about it and answer any questions they have. And limit their viewing if it seems excessive or if it appears to be increasing their stress and anxiety levels. Though it's harder to monitor, also discourage excessive surfing on the Web in search of terrorism reports.

During these uncertain times, one of the most important things you can do for your children is to maintain family routines and traditions. Celebrate holidays and birthdays with all the joy you can muster. Make sure your children eat a balanced diet and get enough sleep. And be sure to carry on the regular activities that have always been part of your lives, whether it's sports, music lessons, religious services, or scouting.

How can I help my kindergarten and elementary-school children?

Young children will hear information about bioterrorism from all kinds of sources—schoolmates, teachers, parents of friends, TV, even snippets of conversations overheard in a store. At this age, they are almost certainly going to misunderstand some of the information and have trouble separating exaggerations and rumors from fact.

They may think terrorists are in their school or believe that something bad happened that didn't. The main thing you need is patience and a willingness to listen. Find out what they've heard, and help them sort through what's real and what's not in a calm, gentle manner.

You may have to reassure them many times about the safety of your family and their school. Tell them the president and many other good people—firefighters, police, military personnel, and medical workers—are working hard to keep us all safe. They may ask you the same questions over and over, which every parent knows can be frustrating. Again, be patient. They may just need to hear the answers several times before they fully understand and accept them.

Children, particularly preadolescent children, may reenact traumatic events as they play (repeatedly wrecking planes and buildings, for example). Such play is often a way for children to attempt to master events that make them feel threatened and helpless.

Reenactments—no matter how uncomfortable for adults— should be encouraged. Young children can often express their feelings and thoughts more fully through play activities than through talking. It may be helpful to provide a special time to paint, draw, or write about the events.

They may also ask what you consider shocking questions seemingly out of the blue. Remember, they're trying to process very confusing and frightening information, and there's no telling when something might pop into their minds. So try to respond in a calm, reassuring way, answering their questions simply and directly. It's important for them to know they can talk with you anytime.

Don't be surprised if you see some regression in young children, including whining, bed-wetting, or needing more help with getting dressed and eating. Be patient and understanding.

And as part of your nightly routine, be sure to tuck them safely into bed and tell them you love them. Sleeping difficulties, especially nightmares, are common. Talk through nightmares with your children, and reassure them about their safety.

How can I help my middle-school children?

To children at this age, the grown-up world can seem scary enough. You may see more aggression in some children, as they try to cover up fears and insecurity with tough talk. And you may see more emotion in others, as they cry and seek reassurance.

Just as this is a time for adults to spend more time with one another, it's important for adolescents to spend more time with their closest friends. Encourage this, even if it means you have to play taxi driver a little more often.

Some middle-school students find it helpful to keep a journal or express what they're feeling through drawing. If they want to share these with you, great. But don't force them to.

It's also possible that middle-school children may talk more about death and dying. Or they may ask questions that include gruesome details or focus on death. This is natural, as they try to comprehend what's happening in the world. Respond calmly. If these comments become persistent, seek professional help.

The main thing parents of middle-school children need to do is be willing to listen. Understand that, on any given day, you may be the last person your child wants to talk to. It's nothing personal.

Think back to when you were their age. How much did you talk to your parents?

But your children will know if you're really interested in what's on their mind. Create a warm, understanding environment for them to share when they're ready.

HOW CAN I HELP MY HIGH-SCHOOL CHILDREN?

Take time to discuss the numerous physical and emotional signs of stress I talked about earlier. This will not only help them understand their own reactions to events but also will teach them important life skills they will need as they prepare to enter the adult world.

Don't talk down to them or try to shelter them from what's going on. They want, and deserve, straight talk from you. For many, the events of September 11 and the months that followed will be forever fixed in their memories.

Without downplaying the tragedy of all those who died, be sure to emphasize the way our country pulled together in a common cause. Talk about all of the people who sacrificed to help others and make a difference.

One of the dangers is that, just as teenagers are about to enter the adult world, it can appear to be a frightening and uninviting place. We can't allow them to grow disillusioned. We owe them a better, brighter future. Talk with them about how world leaders could help reduce hate and violence, and encourage them to get involved in school, religious, or civic organizations.

Many high-school students are searching for, or have only just begun to formulate their own ideas about, what they should believe in. They may have idealistic concepts of right versus wrong, peace versus war, etc.

You may not think so, but as a parent you have a great deal of influence over how your children's beliefs develop. Discuss current events with them, allowing them to raise their own questions about what is right or wrong. As you begin to better understand some of the values your children have started to develop, you will be better able to help guide them.

3

ANTHRAX

ASSESSING THE RISK

Availability HIGH. The anthrax bacterium grows naturally throughout the world, including the United States. There are about two thousand labs in the United States alone that have anthrax samples, not to mention hostile foreign nations such as Iraq that have large supplies. However, obtaining a strain that would do the greatest harm would not be simple.

Stability HIGH. Anthrax spores are highly resistant to drying and to extremes of heat and cold. The spores also are resistant to some disinfectants. Spores can survive in the environment for decades.

Deliverability MEDIUM. It takes technical skill to refine anthrax to the extremely tiny size required to get into the lungs, the staging ground from which it launches its often deadly attack on the body. But as we've learned, someone with that skill can send anthrax though the mail with deadly consequences. Considerably more sophistication would be required to manufacture anthrax for an aerosol release that could inflict mass casualties.

Lethality HIGH. It was thought before the postal attacks that inhalational anthrax would be fatal in 80 to 95 percent of cases. However, six of the eleven people who contracted the disease last fall survived thanks to fast treatment with antibiotics.

Although most Americans knew little about anthrax until recently, the disease has been around at least since biblical times.

Many believe that anthrax fits the description of the fifth "grievous" plague that killed the Egyptians' livestock after

Pharaoh refused to free the Israelites, as recounted in the book of Exodus. Descriptions of similar plagues can be found in the writings of Homer, Virgil, and the ancient Hindus.

But it was the use of the mail to send lethal, anthrax-laced letters to media outlets and government offices last fall that suddenly made this ancient disease a household word. Even now, months after the postal attacks that infected eighteen and killed five, there are a lot of misconceptions about anthrax. For instance, a poll conducted more than a month after the attacks found that a quarter of Americans believed the disease is contagious. It's not. But it's no wonder people are confused. Much of what we know about anthrax as a biological weapon was learned during the attacks last fall.

WHAT IS ANTHRAX?

Anthrax is an infectious disease that can affect both animals and humans. The illness is caused by a spore-forming bacterium called *Bacillus anthracis*. Three forms of anthrax can occur: skin (or in medical terms, cutaneous), inhalational, and gastrointestinal. The form varies based on how the anthrax bacteria enter the body.

The bacterium gets its name from the Greek word for coal, *anthrakis*, because the skin form of the disease—which is by far the most common in humans—is characterized by skin sores that turn coal-black.

Bacillus anthracis can switch back and forth between two states: the active "vegetative" form, and the dormant "spore" form that you've heard so much about. The bacterium is only technically alive when it is in the vegetative state. That's when it can reproduce, take in nutrients, and get rid of wastes. When the bacterium senses a lack of nutrients or water, it dries out and encases itself in a thick, hard shell called a spore that protects it against extreme heat, cold, and even some types of radiation (but not the gamma irradiation currently being used to treat the mail).

In this state of suspended animation, the spores can survive in the soil for decades. That's why anthrax primarily strikes grass-eating animals, such as cattle, goats, sheep, and horses. In fact, viable anthrax spores can still be found along the cattle trails of the Old West.

WHERE IS ANTHRAX FOUND?

Anthrax is not uncommon in agricultural areas of the world, such as Africa and the Middle East. An estimated 20,000 to 100,000 human cases occur globally each year, most of which are skin infections. However, anthrax is rare in industrialized nations such as the United States.

Between 1944 and 1994, just 224 cases of the skin form of the disease were reported in the United States. In the last century, only 18 cases of inhalational anthrax—the most deadly form of the disease—were reported in this country. Two of those cases were related to laboratory work, and not a single inhalational case was reported in the twenty-five years leading up to September 11, 2001.

For thousands of years, the threat of anthrax to humans was primarily limited to farmworkers, woolsorters, and, in rare cases, those who ate tainted meat. That all changed with the postal attacks that followed in the wake of the September 11 terrorist attacks. As of January 1, 2002, 18 newly confirmed cases of anthrax had been identified in the eastern United States and 5 people had died of the disease. This recent outbreak makes it abundantly clear that anthrax can be used as a bioterrorist weapon against civilian populations.

HOW IS ANTHRAX SPREAD?

It's important to note that anthrax is *not* a contagious disease. That means it can't be passed from one person to another. The only way to be infected is to come into direct contact with anthrax spores through one of the ways outlined below.

Humans can contract anthrax several different ways: by directly handling infected animals or contaminated animal products (such as wool or hides); by inhaling anthrax spores into the lungs; and by eating undercooked meat from infected animals. The recent cases from tainted mail demonstrate that infection can also be acquired by handling artificially contaminated items, such as letters or packages.

Handling contaminated animals, animal products, or artificially contaminated items can lead to skin infections. Anthrax spores enter the skin through minor cuts or scrapes; the most frequently infected areas of the body are the arms, hands, face, and neck—the areas most often left exposed. The average time from exposure to onset of illness (the incubation period) for skin infection is one to seven days. Cutaneous anthrax accounts for an overwhelming majority (an estimated 95 percent) of all anthrax cases.

Inhaling the spores can lead to inhalational anthrax. This is the form that concerns us most, because it is the form most likely to be used as a biological weapon and it is the most deadly. Experts believe that the average lethal dose for inhalational anthrax is ten thousand spores, although in view of the recent postal attacks, we now believe that a smaller number can be fatal, especially for the elderly and those with a weakened immune system.

Once inhaled, the microscopically tiny spores—each one less than one-twentieth the diameter of a human hair—lodge in the lungs and then spread to lymph nodes in the middle of the chest between the lungs, in what is known as the mediastinum. The spores convert back to their active vegetative state and begin multiplying with a vengeance.

In hours, or perhaps a few days, a deadly toxin is released that spills over into the bloodstream. Severe shock and death frequently follow. Antibiotics are most successful if begun before the toxins are released.

In the inhalational anthrax cases following September 11, the average time from exposure to the bacteria to the onset of symptoms was four days. But experts believe that illness may occur as long as sixty days after exposure to anthrax spores, because observations have shown that the spores can take that long to change to active bacteria. That explains why preventive (prophylactic) antibiotics are typically given for a sixty-day period. Nonhuman primate studies have suggested that illness may occur up to a hundred days after exposure. This is why after very high exposure to spores, an additional forty days of preventive antibiotics may be recommended.

The third, and least common, way to get anthrax disease is by eating contaminated meat from infected animals. This type of exposure leads to gastrointestinal anthrax, which usually has an incubation period of two to five days.

WHAT ARE THE SYMPTOMS OF ANTHRAX?

Symptoms of anthrax depend on how the disease is contracted. Here's what to look for in each case.

Skin (Cutaneous) Anthrax

Cutaneous anthrax begins as an itchy bump that resembles an insect bite. Within a day or two, it grows into a round, fluid-filled ulcer about a half-inch to a little more than an inch in diameter. A depressed, painless black scab—the characteristic feature of the disease—then forms in the middle of the ulcer. The scab loosens and falls off within one to two weeks, leaving only minimal scarring, if any. Severe swelling may occur around the ulcer and painful swollen lymph nodes may develop in the area. If left untreated, an estimated 20 percent of people will die from cutaneous anthrax. However, with proper antibiotic treatment, the odds of survival are extremely high.

Inhalational Anthrax

The most deadly form of the disease progresses in two distinct stages. The first phase resembles a flulike illness and is marked by fever, chills, headache, nausea, vomiting, muscle aches, and fatigue. Within hours to a few days, during which some patients experience what appears to be a brief period of recovery, the disease moves into its more deadly second stage. This is characterized by high fever, fluid in the lungs, severe breathing problems, and low blood pressure. Massive swelling of lymph nodes in the chest may occur. About half of those with the inhalational form of the disease develop anthrax meningitis if untreated. Left untreated, up to 90 percent of patients may die. However, with early treatment using appropriate antibiotics, the risk of death may be much lower (30 percent). Exciting research on new antitoxin therapy will likely reduce this risk much further in the future.

Gastrointestinal Anthrax

Gastrointestinal anthrax can cause two distinct types of illness. The more common form affects the small or large intestine and resembles a severe case of food poisoning. Initial symptoms include nausea, loss of appetite, vomiting, and fever. These symptoms are quickly followed by abdominal pain, vomiting of blood, and severe diarrhea. A less common form of gastrointestinal anthrax causes a severe sore throat, fever, trouble swallowing, and, sometimes, ulcers in the mouth or back of the throat. Very tender swollen lymph nodes may occur in the neck. If gastrointestinal anthrax is left untreated, about 50 percent of patients will die from the infection.

WHAT DOES IT MEAN WHEN ANTHRAX IS "AEROSOLIZED"?

That simply means it has been made airborne. Anthrax spores naturally tend to clump together in chunks so big that your body's natural mechanical defense system would intercept them before they got deep into the lungs where they cause the biggest problems.

So someone would not only have to be able to refine the particles to microscopically small sizes—an estimated one to five microns in width — but also have enough knowledge to use chemicals to break up the clumps. During this very difficult process, the bacteria can often be rendered inactive.

WHAT DOES IT MEAN WHEN ANTHRAX IS "WEAPONIZED"?

Aerosolizing anthrax is one type of "weaponization," a word that refers to engineering the anthrax spores, either physically or genetically, so they are delivered more efficiently and are more deadly. In the cases following September 11, there was evidence that the anthrax spores had been specially treated so they would remain suspended in the air for prolonged periods, making them more likely to be inhaled because they could literally float out of an envelope.

Another type of weaponization of anthrax, perfected by the Russians in the 1970s, is to engineer it to make it resistant to antibiotics. This fortunately was not the case with the anthrax sent last fall. Given antibiotics' effectiveness against anthrax when used early enough, this is the largest bioterror concern. Other types of weaponization include special milling to refine particle size, adding agents such as stabilizers or skin irritants, and genetic modification to alter the incubation period.

Most experts believe that only a person, a group, or a country with access to advanced biotechnology would be capable of manufacturing and delivering a lethal anthrax aerosol. For example, the

Japanese terrorist group Aum Shinrikyo, which was responsible for the release of deadly Sarin gas in the Tokyo subway system in 1995, had previously tried to disperse aerosolized anthrax and botulism throughout Tokyo on several occasions. For reasons that remain unclear, the attacks caused no illnesses.

CAN ANTHRAX REALLY BE USED AS A WEAPON OF MASS DESTRUCTION?

The answer is yes, though to date it has not been.

Fortunately, it's far more difficult to convert anthrax into a weapon of mass destruction than you may have been led to believe. First, only certain strains of anthrax bacteria are exceptionally deadly. A bioterrorist would have to have access to a particularly virulent strain and then brew a large batch of the microbes. The bacteria would have to be dried and converted to spores, then refined into very, very small particles.

The recent distribution of anthrax through the mail system infected at least eighteen people and killed five The mail system was paralyzed regionally, Congress was essentially shut down for four days, buildings were closed for months. The country was terrorized. But anthrax was not used, as it might have been, as a true weapon of mass destruction. The same amount of anthrax placed in the ventilation system of a building could have exposed thousands to a lethal dose.

For more than three decades, scientific, military, and health experts have tried to analyze the consequences of a large-scale anthrax attack. The worst-case scenario would be that some nation or group was able to spread anthrax from an airplane over a major metropolitan area. In an analysis that is over thirty years old and conducted long before we developed the National Pharmaceutical Stockpile and early-mobilization program, the World

ANTHRAX AS A BIOWEAPON
A Brief History

Research on anthrax as a biological weapon dates back to World War I, when the Germans tried to use it to disrupt the Allies' horse- and reindeer-drawn supply lines across northern Norway. Eighty years later, scientists discovered that a lump of sugar laced with anthrax by a German spy still contained living spores.

During World War II, the United States, fearful that Japan and Germany were making bioweapons, first began experimenting with anthrax and other germ warfare. It was later discovered that Japanese scientists subjected Chinese prisoners of war to horrifying experiments with such lethal bioagents as anthrax, cholera, typhoid, and plague. As many as ten thousand were killed.

The British also conducted anthrax experiments during World War II, detonating explosive shells filled with anthrax spores on an island off the coast of Scotland. The spores were still viable thirty-six years later, and it took an intensive, eight-year decontamination effort requiring 280 tons of formaldehyde and 2,000 tons of seawater to clean up the island.

During the Cold War, the United States and the Soviet Union both undertook extensive bioweapons campaigns that included anthrax. But in 1969, President Richard M. Nixon ended the U.S. offensive biological warfare program and ordered all stockpiled weapons destroyed. In 1972, the United States and more than a hundred nations—including the Soviet Union, Iraq, and Iran—signed the Biological and Toxin Weapons Convention, banning bioweapons.

The Soviets, however, ignored the treaty and geared up their offensive, attack-oriented program. Over seven thousand scientists were involved in this effort. In 1979, anthrax spores were accidentally released into the atmosphere from a secret Soviet military facility in Sverdlovsk. At least seventy-seven people downwind were infected, and sixty-six died.

In the mid-1980s, Iraq launched a bioweapons program and had managed to develop weaponized anthrax by the time of the Gulf War. Iraq reportedly even tested crop-dusting equipment to spread anthrax over a wide area but could not get it to work.

Health Organization estimated in 1970 that the release of aerosolized anthrax over a densely populated area with 5 million people could result in 250,000 casualties, 100,000 of whom would die unless treated.

In another analysis, the U.S. congressional Office of Technology

Assessment (OTA) estimated in 1993 that releasing aerosolized anthrax over Washington, D.C., could result in 130,000 to 3 million deaths—an attack as deadly as a hydrogen bomb. In addition to the horrifying human toll, the economic impact would also be devastating. The Centers for Disease Control and Prevention (CDC) has estimated it would cost the U.S. economy $26.2 billion for every 100,000 people exposed to anthrax.

But, remember, most of these modeling exercises involve assumptions that might not be applicable today. For example, the OTA assessment assumed the attack would not be recognized for six days.

As you'll recall, the government grounded crop dusters for several days in the wake of the September 11 attacks after it was determined that the terrorists had asked questions of a Florida operator. We know that Iraq tested crop-dusting equipment to spray anthrax before the Persian Gulf War, but the effort was unsuccessful. Major modifications would be required to retrofit a plane's sprayer nozzles to spread anthrax in the extremely small, dry particles that would do the most harm.

Again, it would require considerable technical expertise to do this. Dosage and dispersal would be affected by atmospheric conditions, wind, terrain, sun, and other environmental factors. Nevertheless, the impact in terms of terror would be huge.

HOW DO I TELL THE DIFFERENCE BETWEEN THE FLU AND INHALATIONAL ANTHRAX?

The initial stage of inhalational anthrax does resemble the flu (or influenza-like illnesses), but remember, in the winter months, the flu, like the common cold, is a common illness, whereas anthrax is rare and will occur only if you are exposed to the spores. Assume you have the flu unless:

- Anthrax exposure or cases are reported in your community.

- You have reason to believe you have been exposed to anthrax through a suspicious letter or package.

- People around you are suddenly and for no apparent reason coming down with what seems to be the flu or suspicious skin sores. But remember, a cluster of flulike cases is still probably the flu.

Your doctor can give you a quick test for influenza, if you're concerned, though it is not anywhere near 100 percent accurate. That said, there are some subtle differences between anthrax and the flu. Nasal and sinus congestion, sore throat, headache, and a runny nose are common with the flu and the common cold, but not with anthrax. Chest discomfort, vomiting, and shortness of breath are usually associated with anthrax, but not with the flu.

A chest X ray may also be helpful in distinguishing the two. Each of the ten initial patients confirmed to have inhalational anthrax as a result of the recent postal attacks had X-ray abnormalities such as widening of the mediastinum (lymph nodes between the lungs) and fluid around the lungs. You don't typically see these findings with the flu.

It is wise to get a flu shot each year to minimize your chances of catching the flu, and thus lessening the opportunity to even have to think about whether your symptoms might be related to anthrax.

HOW IS ANTHRAX TREATED?

Antibiotics can be quite successful in treating patients who are ill with anthrax. People who have cutaneous anthrax or gastrointestinal anthrax usually can be treated without problems. For antibiotics to be effective in treating inhalational anthrax, it's best if they are given early in the course of illness. Also, the CDC recommends that at least two different antibiotics be used to treat inhalational anthrax.

Antibiotics also can be used to prevent illness after inhalational exposure to anthrax spores. You've probably heard a lot about Cipro (ciprofloxacin) being the top antibiotic choice for preventing anthrax. But doxycycline is equally effective, if the strain of anthrax bacteria involved is not resistant to it.

In fact, as the number of people initially taking ciprofloxacin during the recent postal-related outbreak neared thirty thousand, the CDC switched its preferred recommendation to doxycycline. The change was made in part because of concern that other bacteria would develop resistance to ciprofloxacin with so many people using it.

Doxycycline—which is available in generic form and is about one-tenth the cost of Cipro—was a good alternative under those circumstances. Although recommendations may be modified over the coming months, currently, when no information is available about whether the implicated strain of anthrax bacteria is especially susceptible to any particular antibiotic, ciprofloxacin or doxycycline is recommended for adults and children, although the course for children varies slightly.

Provided the particular strain of anthrax isn't resistant to it, penicillin is recommended by the CDC as another option for the sixty-day course of antibiotics after exposure. However, it is not considered as effective as Cipro or doxycycline for treatment of the disease.

The CDC recommends that preventive treatment with antibiotics continue for sixty days, since it has been shown that the incubation period can be that long. Side effects of treatment with Cipro seen after the anthrax exposure last fall included joint aches and gastrointestinal discomfort in adults. Approximately nine thousand people in Florida, Washington, D.C., New York, and New Jersey were advised to take antibiotics for the full sixty days.

Assessment of side effects and how many people continued the entire sixty-day regimen is under way. And public health experts continue to evaluate how to deal most effectively with anthrax. It may be that, for those individuals with high exposure to airborne anthrax spores, the antibiotic regimen should be extended an additional forty days, just to be on the safe side. And for those at greatest risk of inhalational anthrax, such as those in the room when an anthrax-laden letter is opened, the option of vaccination in addition to antibiotics should be considered.

In response to the events in the Hart Senate Office Building, the CDC in late December of 2001 elected to make anthrax immunization available to the seventy individuals in the immediate vicinity of where the letter was opened.

Currently, the Food and Drug Administration (FDA) has indicated that ciprofloxacin, penicillin G procaine, and doxycycline are approved for preventive treatment following inhalational exposure to anthrax spores. In addition, tetracycline, minocycline, oxytetracycline, demeclocycline, and penicillin G potassium are approved by the FDA for treatment of patients who are clinically ill with anthrax infection.

Every emergency room has plenty of antibiotics on hand for those who need them. Currently, the National Pharmaceutical Stockpile has enough antibiotics to fully treat two million people after an anthrax exposure, and recent federal funding will soon increase that number to millions more. These "push packs" of antibiotics can be made available anywhere in the country within twelve hours.

WHAT ABOUT CHILDREN? IS THERE ANY DIFFERENCE IN THEIR TREATMENT?

For children, the CDC says Cipro and doxycycline can be used for the first two to three weeks of treatment to prevent inhalational anthrax, and for the first one to seven days of treatment for cutaneous anthrax.

The rest of the sixty-day course can be completed with amoxicillin, a form of penicillin that is known for its safety with children and infants, if the organism is sensitive to it. This strategy could avoid potential side effects in children.

The American Academy of Pediatrics generally recommends that doxycycline not be used in children under nine years old because the drug may retard skeletal growth in infants and cause discolored teeth in infants and children. Cipro is not generally recommended for children under the age of sixteen because it may cause temporary joint disease in a small number of children.

However, those potential side effects are greatly outweighed by the serious risk anthrax poses.

WHAT ARE THE SIDE EFFECTS OF CIPRO FOR ADULTS?

Cipro is generally well tolerated. Side effects include vomiting, diarrhea, sun sensitivity, rash, headaches, and dizziness. With prolonged courses of antibiotics, joint aches have been reported. Blurred vision, hypertension, and other nervous system symptoms occur in fewer than 1 percent of patients. Caffeine and medications containing theophylline may accentuate the symptoms.

Each antibiotic has different side effects. Whenever you're prescribed an antibiotic, take time to talk to your physician about the side effects of the specific medicine you are given.

IS THERE A TEST TO SEE IF I'VE BEEN EXPOSED TO ANTHRAX?

Simply put, there is no screening test that determines exposure to anthrax.

We must distinguish between exposure and infection. Exposure is determined by environmental tests; potential exposure is treated with preventive antibiotics. Exposure is not infection. Infection means you have the clinical disease and you need aggressive treatment with antibiotics.

In the opening chapter, I talked about the more than six thousand nasal swab tests that were done on those who were potentially exposed to anthrax spores on Capitol Hill. These tests are best thought of as environmental tests, because all they do is tell where spores have been. They do not detect the presence or absence of *disease* in an individual. They are not like the more familiar throat-culture swabs taken for suspected strep throat, which *are* useful for making treatment decisions for an individual because they detect whether or not that person has a disease.

Nasal swabs are typically used to determine how far spores have traveled in a specific room or building where the presence of anthrax is suspected or has already been established by environmental sampling. They are useful only for public health officials to define the perimeter of potential exposure. At the current time, recommendations for preventive antibiotics are made on the basis of probable exposure.

So no one should request a nasal swab thinking it will change his or her personal care.

To determine actual infection or disease (not just exposure), there is a blood culture test that's accurate and definitive. It involves placing a blood sample in a culture of nutrients and then waiting twenty-four to seventy-two hours to see if an anthrax colony grows. The lack of a fast, accurate, simple test to determine infection is one of the challenges we face. Promising new technology is on the horizon, however.

Scientists are developing a test that would use DNA technology similar to that used in criminal investigations and genetic tests to deliver accurate results within just two to three hours. And there is some indication that radio imaging used to detect infections may be able to be adapted so it picks up signs of anthrax infections before they spread to the bloodstream. Best of all, the test would take only forty-five minutes. As noted earlier, early diagnosis and treatment—ideally before onset of symptoms—may play an important role in saving the lives of those who contract inhalational anthrax.

SHOULD I TAKE ANTIBIOTICS "JUST IN CASE"?

The short answer is no. To begin with, the antibiotics used to treat anthrax carry serious side effects for some people. There's no reason to subject yourself to them unless there is a real risk of disease.

Even more important, if you take antibiotics when you don't actually need them, there's a chance they won't work if and when you do. Bacteria are cagey, versatile, and always changing. When exposed to antibiotics for prolonged periods, the bacteria self-select and become resistant to that antibiotic and even to related antibiotics. That creates a very real potential danger for you and for others because there may be no treatment for future disease caused by that self-selected, resistant bacteria.

SHOULD I STOCKPILE A SIXTY-DAY SUPPLY OF CIPRO OR DOXYCYCLINE?

It's not a good idea to stockpile antibiotics. They have a specific shelf life, and it's possible the antibiotics would expire before you needed them. Plus, if many people hoard the antibiotics, it creates the possibility that there could be a shortage if they actually were needed somewhere.

Many would be tempted to take the drugs unnecessarily, opening up the potential for side effects and the Pandora's box of poten-

tially resistant, deadly bacteria—not only for themselves, but for
society as a whole.

SHOULD I BE VACCINATED FOR ANTHRAX?

There is an anthrax vaccine, which, according to the CDC, is recommended for people aged eighteen years and older who have a
high likelihood of coming into contact with anthrax spores. These
include military personnel; certain laboratory workers; people
whose jobs may expose them to anthrax, such as those who work
with animal products from areas of the world where disease in animals is common; and veterinarians who may handle potentially
infected animals (again, in areas of the world where anthrax is
common).

In addition, last December for the first time, the vaccine was
offered to those who had high direct exposure to the anthrax in our
mail system.

The vaccine is in extremely short supply, and it is not available
to the general public. Currently, only one small company in
Michigan is licensed to produce the vaccine. But a large-scale vaccination program really isn't called for, considering the enormous
cost and difficult logistics, coupled with the low probability of an
attack in any given community. Remember, even with the postal
attacks last fall, the odds of any one person contracting anthrax are
much less than those of getting struck by lightning or attacked by
a shark.

Also, the current vaccine is given in a series of six shots over
eighteen months, and a yearly booster shot is also recommended.
It is known to protect against skin infection and is believed to be
effective against inhaled spores as well. About a third of those who
get the vaccine experience tenderness and redness in the area of
the shot. More severe reactions are infrequent.

Promising new vaccines are being developed, and one of our

top priorities in safeguarding our nation against possible anthrax attacks is to develop, manufacture, and stockpile a new generation of vaccine. Last December, the CDC acquired 220,000 doses from the Pentagon to investigate how best to use the current vaccine in the meantime. Vaccinating all the people considered potentially at risk today for occupational reasons would require at least 28,000 doses.

SHOULD I BE AFRAID TO OPEN MY MAIL?

Until as recently as October 2001, experts believed that there was little threat posed by letters coming in contact with anthrax-laced mail or going through postal machinery that handled contaminated letters. But the mysterious anthrax-related deaths of an elderly woman in Connecticut and another woman in New York in cases seemingly unconnected to the postal attacks forced them to reevaluate that stance.

The probe showed that other mail containing faint traces of anthrax had been delivered to addresses near both victims, leading investigators to believe that cross-contaminated mail may have been delivered to the victims. Only trace amounts of anthrax, much less than experts believed would be needed to harm people, were found on the other letters.

Even if cross-contaminated mail was responsible for the two deaths, it's important to remember that tens of thousands of letters went through the same postal sorting machines at about the same time without causing illness. It's now believed that the elderly and people with weakened immune systems may be at a higher risk from cross-contaminated mail. But it's important to keep in mind that the risk is still very, very low.

A little caution will go a long way here. There is no need to wear a mask and gloves to open your personal mail. If you're concerned about your personal mail, the CDC offers these simple recommendations:

- Avoid holding letters to your nose or sniffing them before opening.

- Don't shake or jostle the contents.

- Wash your hands thoroughly after handling mail.

WHEN SHOULD I BE SUSPICIOUS OF A LETTER OR PACKAGE?

A letter or package should be considered suspicious if it is not addressed to a specific person; is marked with such restrictions as "Personal," "Confidential," or "Do not X-ray"; or is postmarked from a city or state that doesn't match the return address. In addition, exercise caution if the letter or package has excessive postage, misspellings of common words, a strange return address or no return address, a handwritten or poorly typed address, or incorrect titles or a title without a name.

Other suspicious signs include a powdery substance felt through or appearing on the package or envelope, oily stains, discolorations, or odor, a lopsided or uneven envelope, or excessive packaging material, such as masking tape or string.

If a package or letter appears suspicious, don't open it, shake it, or carry it around to show others. Simply put it down on a stable surface. Do not sniff it, touch it, or look too closely at it. Immediately leave the area and make sure anyone else present leaves, too. Shut the door and immediately turn off the ventilation system.

Ensure that all persons who touched the piece of mail wash their hands with soap and water immediately or as soon as possible, and call 911 (or local law enforcement officials). If feasible, place all items worn when you were in contact with the suspected mail piece in plastic bags and have them available for law enforcement agents. As soon as practical, shower with soap and water.

If possible, create a list of persons who were in the room or area when the suspicious letter or package was recognized and a list of persons who may also have handled the package or letter. Give the list to both the local public health authorities and law enforcement officials.

HOW IS ANTHRAX DETECTED IN A BUILDING?

Testing environmental samples—taken from furniture, mailboxes, and ventilation ducts, for example—is complex and painstaking. It's also very accurate and critically important to determine where and how far anthrax has spread.

At the height of the postal-related outbreak last fall, the CDC looked at more than twenty-five hundred specimens, not just from New York and Washington, but from all over the country. The CDC is to be commended for rising to the challenge. It usually has about ten scientists working on anthrax-related issues, but in response to the mail attacks, it had eighty scientists working seven days a week on the case. It also provided laboratory support to field sites in Florida, New York, Washington, D.C., and New Jersey.

Typically, specimens such as envelopes suspected of anthrax contamination are taken to a biohazard lab, where they are opened under a special hood that sucks air away from the technicians and through powerful filters to keep spores from becoming airborne. The samples are then dissolved or soaked in water, and testing, which includes microscopic examination, culture, and genetic analysis, begins. For safety reasons, technicians working with the samples wear protective gloves, special disposable waterproof gowns, and N95 masks, which filter out tiny particles.

WE'VE ALL SEEN THE PICTURES OF PEOPLE WEARING "SPACE SUITS" AT THE SITES OF ANTHRAX CONTAMINATION. WHAT ARE THEY WEARING?

They are wearing disposable protective clothing that primarily protects the skin but also eliminates the likelihood of transferring contamination to other sites. Their respiratory devices are powered, air-purifying respirators, with full-face masks that allow them a full field of vision and are equipped with high-efficiency particulate air (HEPA) filters. Wearing a powered, air-purifying respirator with a full-face mask that has been specifically fitted to the wearer will reduce inhalation exposures by 98 percent. The disposable gloves, which are made of lightweight nitrile or vinyl, provide protection but preserve dexterity. A thin cotton glove is frequently worn under the disposable glove to protect against skin rash, which can occur when hands naturally perspire while inside gloves for prolonged periods.

HOW IS A BUILDING DECONTAMINATED AFTER ANTHRAX HAS BEEN DISCOVERED?

There is no established protocol, or detailed procedure, for decontamination of buildings, and indeed the effort has proved far more complex than anyone would have anticipated. The anthrax release in the Hart Senate Office Building in Washington that I chronicled in the opening chapter provides the best example.

The building remained closed for almost three months as the best scientists and environmental experts in the world oversaw the cleanup. The entire building was closed on October 17, after twenty-eight workers tested positive for exposure. More than half of all senators had to relocate to temporary offices.

On December 1, six weeks after the incident, Sen. Thomas Daschle's suite, where the anthrax-laced letter was opened, was sealed and filled with a high concentration of chlorine dioxide gas. When traces of anthrax were found in 9 of 377 environmental samples taken afterward, the Environmental Protection Agency decided to go back in and fumigate again.

This time, they used the chlorine dioxide gas in the ventilation system in those sections of the building where traces of anthrax were found and the liquid form of chlorine dioxide in the office suite itself. Afterward, a second chemical, sodium bisulfite, was used to break down the gas. One of the problems in deciding when a contaminated building is ready to reopen is that there is no agreed-upon standard of how many anthrax spores constitute a health threat.

Computers, files, and books from the suite were packed up and taken to a company in Richmond, Virginia, for treatment with ethylene oxide, which is commonly used to sanitize medical instruments.

In eleven other senators' offices in the building, liquid and foam forms of the chlorine dioxide and particle-filtering vacuums were used.

4

SMALLPOX

One of the greatest medical and public health accomplishments of the past century was the eradication of smallpox from the world. That means most Americans have never had to live with the threat of this devastating disease.

But in recent years, it has reemerged in a new guise: as the scariest bioterrorism nightmare. The reintroduction of smallpox into today's world could be catastrophic. While the odds are remote that it could happen, we must be prepared. The stakes are simply too high.

WHAT IS SMALLPOX?

Smallpox is an infection caused by the variola virus. The virus comes in two forms: variola major and variola minor. Smallpox caused by variola major often is fatal; in the last century alone, smallpox claimed the lives of five hundred million people. Even as recently as the 1950s, an estimated fifty million cases of smallpox occurred in the world each year. But, in probably the most successful public health effort ever, smallpox disease has been eradicated from the face of the earth! There is no smallpox disease— anywhere.

HOW DID WE WIPE OUT SMALLPOX?

Smallpox has been recognized as a scourge for thousands of years. Ancient writings describe a disease that resembles smallpox as early as 1122 B.C. in China, and it also appears in ancient Sanskrit texts from India. Pharaoh Ramses V apparently died of smallpox in 1157 B.C. The disease swept through Japan and Korea, reaching Europe in A.D. 710.

The explorer Hernando Cortés brought smallpox to the Americas in 1520, and 3.5 million Aztecs died in the next two years. In the eighteenth century, smallpox reached epidemic proportions in Europe, killing every seventh child born in Russia and every tenth child born in Sweden and France. Even royalty offered no protection against the disease, which claimed the lives of Queen Mary II of England, Emperor Joseph I of Austria, King Louis I of Spain,

Czar Peter II of Russia, Queen Ulrika Eleonora of Sweden, and King Louis XV of France.

In 1798, however, an English country doctor named Edward Jenner proved that inoculation with a related but nonfatal virus called cowpox could protect against smallpox, offering hope for the first time that the disease could be stemmed. As vaccination became more widespread, the tide began to turn. Eventually, the cowpox vaccine was replaced by one made with the vaccinia virus, which produced fewer side effects.

In 1967, the World Health Organization (WHO) launched an ambitious program to wipe out smallpox. Mass vaccination campaigns were carried out throughout the world, and outbreaks were carefully contained. Through famine, flood, cholera, and civil war, the vaccination program pushed forward until victory was won.

The last naturally occurring case of smallpox was recorded in October 1977 in Somalia. In 1980, the WHO declared that naturally occurring smallpox had been eradicated and recommended a worldwide end to vaccinations. The last smallpox case in the United States was in 1949, and vaccinations here were halted in 1972.

How is smallpox spread?

Smallpox is spread primarily through respiratory droplets, or aerosols, from infected patients. A person generally becomes infectious, or capable of spreading the disease to others, once the rash starts. And smallpox patients are most infectious during the first week of illness, when lesions in the mouth ulcerate, releasing substantial amounts of the virus into the saliva.

Those with smallpox remain infectious until all of the lesions on their bodies have scabbed over and the scabs have fallen off. Usually, the virus is spread through droplets, and only those who come within about six and a half feet of an infectious person—what we would consider face-to-face contact—are considered at risk. In rare instances, some patients produce fine aerosols and the infection is more communicable. Examples include infectious patients with a bad cough or those with the severe, hemorrhagic form of the disease. Contaminated clothing or bedding also can spread the virus.

In past outbreaks, the average smallpox patient infected five other people. If there were an outbreak today, it's estimated that that number could be as high as ten new infections per smallpox patient, since our population is considered even more highly susceptible, especially in light of increased mobility.

WHAT ARE THE SYMPTOMS OF SMALLPOX?

Smallpox has an incubation period (time from exposure to onset of illness) of seven to seventeen days. The first symptoms—high fever, fatigue, headache, severe prostration (physical collapse), and backache—usually appear twelve to fourteen days after exposure. The distinctive rash, or pox, usually breaks out two to three days later.

The rash first develops as tiny pink spots in the throat and mouth and typically spreads to the face and forearms, then to the trunk and legs. The rash is densest on the face and extremities. A distinctive characteristic of smallpox is that the rash occurs on the palms of the hands and soles of the feet. In addition, delirium strikes about 15 percent of smallpox patients. The rash grows into vesicles, or small raised bumps, that often contain fluid and within several days become filled with pus. The lesions can be extremely painful. About eight or nine days after the rash first appears, scabs start to form. Once the scabs fall off, people often are left with pitted scarring, especially on the face.

The illness caused by variola minor, which was first identified in the early 1900s, tends to be less severe, with fewer skin lesions and milder symptoms. Also, people who have some residual immunity from past vaccinations may have milder symptoms and may recover more quickly.

Occasionally, unusual forms of smallpox can occur: hemorrhagic smallpox and malignant smallpox. In the hemorrhagic form, bleeding into the skin and from mucous membranes occurs. In the malignant form, the rash remains flat and does not develop into the pus-filled form that is usually seen. Both forms are almost always fatal.

COULD SMALLPOX REALLY BE USED AS A BIOLOGICAL WEAPON?

The threat must be taken very seriously. All we need to do is look at the deadly swath smallpox has cut through history to understand how formidable a viral foe it is. And although the disease is gone, the virus that causes it still exists.

After the disease was eradicated, the WHO urged all laboratories to destroy their stocks of the variola virus that causes smallpox or to transfer them to one of the two WHO-approved research labs: the Centers for Disease Control and Prevention (CDC) in Atlanta and the Institute of Virus Preparations in Moscow. Because only two labs in the world are authorized to warehouse the smallpox virus, would-be bioterrorists will likely find it exceedingly difficult to get their hands on it.

But it's suspected that nations with bioterror programs, including Iraq and North Korea, may have gained access to the virus, increasing the likelihood that it could fall into the hands of terrorists. And it's known that Russia in the 1980s secretly, and in violation of an international treaty, produced more than twenty tons of smallpox virus specifically for use in bombs and intercontinental ballistic missiles.

However, unlike other possible bioterror agents such as anthrax, botulism, and tularemia, there are no natural stores of smallpox in the soil or animals. Nor does smallpox have the ability to form spores, the hard shells that protect anthrax and botulism bacteria indefinitely in a state of suspended animation.

The technical expertise required to engineer smallpox as a bioweapon is higher than that needed to weaponize anthrax. And even if there are secret stocks stashed away, it's unlikely they would willingly be turned over to terrorists because the disease is so contagious and difficult to control. The risk is extremely high that any group or nation that unleashes this dreaded disease on the world would also inflict it on its own people.

But as unlikely as a smallpox attack seems, we must be prepared for it because the potential results could be devastating. The virus can be aerosolized, is infectious in a relatively small amount, and would quickly spread over a wide area if it is released in cool, dry weather, particularly in winter. Smallpox is highly contagious, and our population is highly vulnerable to it because nobody has been vaccinated or exposed to the disease here in thirty years.

Last year, the military held an exercise called Dark Winter, in which a simulated smallpox attack was unleashed on the United States. The simulation started with 20 confirmed cases in Oklahoma City. Within just two weeks, the disease had spread like wildfire. There were 16,000 reported cases in twenty-five states, with 1,000 deaths. And smallpox outbreaks were reported in ten other countries. In another three weeks, it was estimated that there would be as many as 300,000 total victims, with 100,000 deaths. And within two months, there would be an estimated 3 million smallpox cases and up to 1 million deaths.

Although this exercise was just a simulation, the grim scenario that it predicted was a wake-up call, and steps have already been taken to fix many of the problems identified during the Dark Winter exercise. But the exercise illustrates just how dangerous a threat smallpox poses to a highly vulnerable and very mobile people.

COULD TERRORISTS TURN THEMSELVES INTO "BIOLOGICAL SUCIDE BOMBERS," DELIBERATELY INFECTING THEMSELVES WITH SMALLPOX AND THEN SPREADING THE DISEASE IN A CROWDED AREA?

It is possible. But remember, smallpox patients generally become infectious once the characteristic rash develops. By that time, they typically already have a high fever, fatigue, headache, severe prostration, and backache. In other words, they're thoroughly miserable and weak. Add to that the fact that, if they wanted the best chance to spread the disease, they would have to wait until the rash had fully erupted.

It would be difficult for people with this advanced stage of the illness to walk at all, and even more difficult to walk undetected through a crowded mall or sporting event. And the infected individuals would have to get within about six feet of others to even have a chance of spreading the disease. But the unthinkable can happen.

IS SMALLPOX ALWAYS FATAL?

No. Before the disease was eradicated, the death rate among unvaccinated persons for the most serious form, variola major, was about 30 percent. Variola minor kills only about 1 percent of its victims.

The vaccinia vaccine can offer protection for previously unvaccinated persons exposed to the smallpox virus, provided it's given one to three days—and perhaps even as long as four days—after exposure. People who are vaccinated soon after they are exposed may not fall ill, or if they do, the disease is usually less severe and not likely to be fatal. For this reason, early diagnosis is critical. Early vaccination is critical. Every moment counts.

IF I WAS VACCINATED AGAINST SMALLPOX BEFORE 1972, AM I
STILL PROTECTED?

Not really.

At best, if you were vaccinated thirty or more years ago, you
would only have partial immunity at this point. It's uncertain how
much. Some experts estimate that a single dose of smallpox vaccine
offers protection for probably three to five years, and not more
than ten years. Since routine smallpox vaccinations ended in the
United States in 1972, that means our entire population must be
considered highly vulnerable.

Anyone exposed to the virus now would have to be vaccinated
again, regardless of whether he had been vaccinated as a child. It's

---

SMALLPOX AS A BIOWEAPON
A Brief History

An outbreak of smallpox on the Pennsylvania frontier in 1763 led to the first docu-
mented case of the use of smallpox as a bioweapon. The outbreak occurred among the
British forces at Fort Pitt, on the site that would later become Pittsburgh.

Sir Jeffrey Amherst, commander of British forces in North America, ordered that blankets and handkerchiefs used by smallpox patients in the fort's infirmary be given to the
Delaware Indians in a deliberate attempt to reduce their numbers. A smallpox epidemic
swept through Native American tribes in the Ohio River valley, although it's unlikely that the
contaminated items were the sole cause, since there was other contact between colonists
and Native Americans at the time.

The use of smallpox as a weapon has been rare in history, and for good reason. It is
very difficult to control, and the disease is so contagious, it would almost certainly come
back to victimize those who unleashed it. But that didn't deter the Soviet Union from trying to harness it as a weapon of mass destruction.

We know that the Soviets produced tons of smallpox virus in the 1980s for use in cluster bombs and intercontinental ballistic missiles. One of our greatest concerns now is that
some of the scientists who worked in that terrifying program may sell their services and
products to our enemies.

That's one of the reasons we need to be prepared for a potential attack, regardless of
how remote the odds seem.

possible, however, that a revaccination for someone who was immunized as a child might boost immunity faster than a first-time vaccination. Where possible, the CDC will revaccinate health care workers and emergency personnel first so they could handle patients during the early stages of a smallpox outbreak.

IS THERE ENOUGH VACCINE TO COVER EVERYONE?

There will be by the end of 2002. The United States had 15.4 million doses of smallpox vaccine on hand at the time of the September 11 attacks. Preliminary testing suggests that the existing doses can be diluted to create five doses each, which will bring the current supply to 77 million doses. Following the terrorist attacks, the United States immediately ordered an additional 54 million doses from a Massachusetts-based company. To cover the rest of our citizens, President Bush last November signed a contract with a British firm to buy 155 million more doses, at a cost of $428 million. By the end of 2002, we will have 286 million doses on hand, enough to protect every man, woman, and child in our nation if it is ever deemed necessary.

WHY DON'T WE JUST DESTROY THE REMAINING SMALLPOX VIRUS WE HAVE? WOULDN'T THAT DECREASE THE ODDS OF ITS BEING USED AGAINST US?

If it weren't for the threat of bioterrorism, we might have been able to be forever rid of smallpox. The WHO has long advocated destroying the remaining stocks of smallpox virus, and the United States had been expected to kill off its remaining supplies this year. But the Bush administration correctly reversed that decision in the wake of the September 11 attacks. As anxious as we are to eliminate the possibility that smallpox will be reintroduced in the world, we now need the remaining stocks to help develop an arsenal of drugs to keep us safe.

Given the fact that Russian scientists succeeded in turning smallpox into a weapon of mass destruction, and the chance that rogue nations may have illegal supplies, we must act prudently. The administration wants to develop at least two antiviral drugs, a vaccine that everyone can take safely, and diagnostic tests and environmental detectors to remove this threat once and for all.

It's regrettable that, given the misery this disease has caused and the triumph of medicine over this ancient scourge, we cannot now take the final step of destroying the remaining research stocks of the virus. But clearly it would be unwise to kill off our supplies when we don't know who else might have the smallpox virus and when we still don't have a vaccine that's safe for everyone or any effective treatment once the disease strikes.

WHY DOESN'T THE GOVERNMENT JUST VACCINATE EVERYONE?

First of all, we don't have enough vaccine on hand right now to vaccinate everyone. But even when we do by the end of the year, the risk of side effects from vaccination outweighs the benefits of vaccination when the virus is not circulating in the population. The decision to vaccinate our population against a particular disease should be made when:

- People have a relatively high likelihood of being exposed to the disease; in other words, the virus is circulating in the population.

- The disease is likely to spread from person to person.

- The effects of vaccination are not worse than the actual disease.

On the basis of our experiences from the 1950s and 1960s, we would predict that if we were to revaccinate the entire country of almost 300 million people for smallpox, at least 1,500 people would develop a serious side effect from the vaccine and at least 300 people would likely die. The most common side effects, listed from most to least serious, along with their rates of occurrence as determined by a 1968 study, include:

- Postvaccinial encephalitis (12.3 cases per million vaccinations). Between eight and fifteen days after vaccination, symptoms related to inflammation of the brain develop. These symptoms include fever, headache, vomiting, drowsiness, and, sometimes, paralysis, signs of meningitis, coma, and convulsions. One in four people who developed postvaccinial encephalitis died.

- Progressive vaccinia (1.5 cases per million vaccinations). This rare reaction is often fatal for those with weakened immune systems. The lesions from the vaccination fail to heal, killing adjacent skin tissue, then spreading to other parts of the skin, bones, and internal organs.

- Eczema vaccinatum (38.5 cases per million vaccinations). The vaccination causes the spread of eczema, an itching inflammation of the skin with lesions.

- Generalized vaccinia (241.5 cases per million vaccinations). About six to nine days after vaccination, lesions—caused by the virus being disseminated through the blood—erupt. This complication typically cleared up on its own.

- Inadvertent inoculation (529.2 cases per million vaccinations). Lesions are spread from one person to another through close contact, or to other parts of the person's own body such as the face, eyelid, mouth, and genitalia. Most lesions healed on their own.

Historically, about one death occurs for every 1 million people who receive a first-time vaccination, and about one death occurs for every 4 million who are revaccinated.

These predictions may underestimate the side effects because today our population includes hundreds of thousands more people with weakened immune systems (many of whom don't know it), including people with HIV infection, people taking drugs to suppress rejection of organ transplants, and those being treated for cancer. These people are at greater risk of serious side effects and death following vaccination. Inadvertent vaccination of some people who do not know they have weakened immune systems would likely increase the rate of serious side effects and death.

Also, the CDC recommends that an injection of a medicine known as vaccinia immune globulin (VIG) be given to those who develop a serious side effect. Since VIG currently is in short supply, the number of people who could die after developing a serious side effect may actually be higher than historic estimates. In addition, up to 70 percent of all children who get the smallpox vaccine have a fever of 100 degrees or higher for one or two days, and 15 to 20 percent would have fever above 102 degrees.

Routine smallpox vaccinations were discontinued thirty years ago because the risk of serious side effects from vaccination was considered to be greater than the risk of disease. Because it is far from certain that anyone will actually ever be exposed to smallpox, the risk of killing hundreds of Americans and making many more ill through vaccination outweighs the potential benefits of using the vaccine at this time.

Even if smallpox were deliberately released, vaccination within three days after exposure protects almost completely against the disease. Vaccinating exposed people as late as four days after exposure may still protect against severe symptoms and death.

These are the recommendations as of 2002. They may be changed as new vaccines are developed and risks of exposure to virus are modified.

HOW HARD IS IT TO ACCURATELY DIAGNOSE SMALLPOX?

Because no cases of smallpox have been seen in the United States for a long time, doctors are not familiar with the illness and there is no easy test to help make the diagnosis. The initial symptoms and rash of smallpox can easily be confused with chicken pox, which is caused by a different virus and is much milder and rarely fatal.

However, there are some subtle differences that can be used to distinguish between the two diseases soon after illness strikes. The chicken pox rash itches, while the lesions of smallpox can be quite painful. The smallpox rash tends to appear within one or two days after the onset of illness, and the lesions all erupt and evolve at the same rate. Chicken pox lesions are much more superficial, pop up in groups every few days—we say they occur in "crops"—and evolve at different rates. Also, chicken pox tends not to concentrate on the face, arms, and legs, and it's almost never found on the palms of the hands or soles of the feet.

If smallpox is suspected, samples of fluid from skin lesions can be tested for the virus. However, testing can be performed only in highly specialized laboratories that have adequate protective equipment and procedures in place.

HOW WOULD A SMALLPOX OUTBREAK BE CONTAINED?

The CDC plan is basically quite simple: Identify those with small-pox, isolate them to keep them from infecting others, and vaccinate anyone with whom they may have come into contact. The

WHO has recently gone on record supporting this approach as the best method to stop a smallpox outbreak.

Once someone is diagnosed with smallpox, the key to containing an outbreak is to vaccinate everyone who has been in close contact with the victim after the onset of the rash. This strategy is called "ring vaccination." Close contact usually means family and friends, since generally the virus is only spread to those people who have been within about six feet of an infected person during the time that the rash is present.

Often by the time the rash has erupted and a person is infectious, he or she is severely ill and is home in bed. Once infected people are identified through their health care providers, investigators would interview them to identify others who likely were exposed to the virus in the previous three weeks. Health officials would then track down those people and immediately vaccinate them.

In the wake of the September 11 attacks, the CDC vaccinated about 140 members of special teams of disease detectives who are ready to be sent at a moment's notice to investigate a suspected outbreak anywhere in the country. In addition, the CDC has been training local and state health officials to prepare them to respond to a potential smallpox outbreak.

WHO WOULD GET VACCINATED FIRST DURING AN OUTBREAK?

If an outbreak is confirmed, the CDC can have sufficient vaccine delivered within twelve hours. Those receiving the vaccination first would likely include:

- Anyone exposed to the initial release of the virus, provided the release was discovered during the first generation of cases at a time when vaccination would still be of benefit, or within four days after exposure.

- Anyone who had face-to-face contact with a smallpox patient after fever set in, including all those in the same household. Although a smallpox patient is not infectious until the rash appears, this approach provides a buffer and assures that people who potentially were exposed will be vaccinated.

- Public health, medical, and emergency personnel who care for or transport smallpox patients.

- Lab personnel who work with specimens from patients.

- Workers who are likely to handle infectious materials, including those involved in disposing of medical waste or linens, or disinfecting bedding and rooms.

- Personnel involved in tracing contacts and vaccination, isolation enforcement, or law enforcement interviews of suspected smallpox patients.

- Persons permitted to enter any facilities designated for the evaluation, treatment, or isolation of confirmed or suspected smallpox patients.

- Persons present in a facility with a smallpox case where fine-particle aerosol transmission was likely, such as a patient with an active cough or the hemorrhagic form of the disease.

WOULD I HAVE TO STAND IN LINE FOR HOURS TO GET VACCINATED IF THERE WERE AN OUTBREAK?

If the outbreak is relatively small, it's possible that public health employees would administer the vaccinations in people's homes.

But if the outbreak grows too large, the vaccinations likely would be given in a staging area, such as a school. Mass vaccination of a community's entire population would only be undertaken if the virus were released in the air in a crowded area or if public health officials deemed that mass vaccination was needed to control the outbreak.

The CDC, however, will not force people to be vaccinated against their will. And that's the right decision. The last thing we would need is people trying to flee to avoid vaccination, undermining public confidence, creating chaos, and potentially spreading the virus even farther.

WOULD THE GOVERNMENT HAVE TO QUARANTINE PEOPLE DURING A SMALLPOX OUTBREAK?

Because the key to containing any outbreak is isolating those infected, special quarters might have to be set up to quarantine people if hospitals can't handle everyone who needs care.

This would be done in what the CDC designates as type C isolation facilities. These would include any empty building or building not used for other purposes, such as a motel, a dedicated hospital or a separate building of a hospital, or a college dormitory. To be considered as an isolation ward, the building must have its own air-conditioning, heating, and ventilation systems that exhaust 100 percent of air to the outside through a HEPA filter, or else be at least a hundred yards from any other occupied buildings or area.

The building also must have adequate water, electricity, a dependable communications system, and the ability to support the wide range of medical care that will be needed, including IVs, oxygen machines, vital-signs monitors, ventilators to aid breathing, radiology, and basic laboratory tests.

Everyone who enters a type C facility *must* be vaccinated.

WHAT ARE THE CHANCES THAT AN EFFECTIVE SMALLPOX CURE WILL SOON BE DISCOVERED?

It looks fairly promising, although more research is needed. In fact, we may already have a cure and not know it. That's because medicine has advanced tremendously since smallpox was eradicated more than twenty years ago. It seems hard to believe today, but at that time there were no drugs that could combat a virus—any virus. Now we have medicines that effectively work against AIDS, herpes, influenza, and some other viral illnesses. So it's certainly possible that antiviral medicines that have been developed for other purposes may work against smallpox. In fact, twenty-one drugs have already shown that they can kill the virus in a test tube. Whether any of those will work in people is the question we must answer.

The most promising medication to date is cidofovir, or Vistide, which is used to treat eye infections caused by cytomegalovirus, a complication seen in some people with AIDS. The biggest problem is that cidofovir is only available by injection, not in pill form, which would make it difficult to use under emergency conditions. However, studies are under way to come up with at least two orally administered drugs that can treat smallpox by completely different biological means. In addition, work is ongoing to study the virus's nearly two hundred genes for clues about how strains vary. This scientific detective work could be crucial if a bioterror attack uses a genetically modified strain of smallpox to make it more dangerous.

5

PLAGUE

ASSESSING THE RISK

Availability MEDIUM. The *Yersinia pestis* bacterium that causes plague is stored in microbe banks around the world. But safeguards would make it difficult to acquire a powerful strain.

Stability MEDIUM. Plague bacteria are sensitive to sunlight, heat, and disinfectants. It's estimated that the bacteria would remain viable and infectious for up to one hour if released into the air.

Deliverability MEDIUM. The Soviets demonstrated that the bacteria could be mass-produced as a potential weapon. But the degree of technical sophistication required is very high.

Lethality VERY HIGH. Unless treated quickly with antibiotics, pneumonic plague, the form most likely to be used by bioterrorists, kills almost 100 percent of the time. Overall, the death rate is 57 percent.

Plague. The very name—which literally means to strike or hit—conjures deep-rooted fears that date back centuries. It's understandable why: In the fourteenth century, the Black Death was responsible for killing a greater proportion of the world's population than any other disease or war in history.

Sadly, we can't consign this deadly disease to the pages of a history book. Hundreds of tons of plague bacteria were produced during the Cold War as a potential bioweapon. It is indeed a possible, though highly unlikely, bioterror threat.

WHAT IS PLAGUE?

There are different kinds of plague, but they're all caused by a bacterium called *Yersinia pestis*. The disease is transmitted to humans by the bite of a flea that has fed on an infected rodent.

A single fleabite can inject thousands of tiny organisms into the skin, where they make a beeline for the nearest lymph nodes. What happens next determines the specific form of plague a person contracts.

WHAT IS BUBONIC PLAGUE?

This is the most common naturally occurring form of the disease. It's also the kind believed responsible for the Black Death. Once the plague bacteria reach the lymph nodes, they multiply rapidly, causing the lymph nodes to grow swollen and tender.

These swollen lymph nodes are called buboes, giving bubonic plague its name. Because fleabites are most common on the legs and arms, the lymph nodes in the groin and armpits are most commonly involved.

WHAT OTHER KINDS OF PLAGUE ARE THERE?

In cases where the bacteria are not contained by the lymph nodes, they enter the bloodstream, where they can affect many different organ systems. This is known as septicemic plague.

When they travel to the lungs and launch an attack there, pneumonia can develop. This is what is known as pneumonic plague. Unlike the bubonic form, which can be treated effectively with antibiotics, pneumonic plague is extremely lethal; about half of patients diagnosed with this form of plague die even with antibiotics and the support of modern intensive medical care. And to make matters worse, pneumonic plague is highly contagious, spread person-to-person when coughing expels the bacteria into the air.

It is the ability of the bacteria to cause severe pneumonia and spread from person to person that underscores the threat we face. It's believed that the most likely bioterror scenario would involve releasing plague bacteria into the air over a densely populated area, where it would be inhaled by thousands, who may then spread it to others.

In an outbreak of plague that results from such a scenario, many people would develop severe respiratory symptoms and pneumonia over a relatively short period of time. This would present a very different pattern from a naturally occurring outbreak of plague and could initially be mistaken for an outbreak of influenza.

WHAT ARE THE SYMPTOMS OF PLAGUE?

The symptoms depend on the form of plague a person contracts. Since pneumonic plague is the form most likely to result from a bioterror attack, we'll deal with it first.

Following an aerosol or airborne exposure, the disease progresses extremely quickly, which is one of the main challenges it poses. Like most diseases, the earlier plague is diagnosed and treated, the more likely the infection can be controlled and the potential for an epidemic minimized.

The incubation period—the interval between exposure and the development of symptoms—can range from one to six days, but the first signs and symptoms are usually seen within two to four days from the time the plague bacteria is inhaled. These include fever, fatigue, and a cough with bloody or watery sputum, a mixture of saliva and mucus. Nausea, vomiting, stomach pain, and diarrhea also are frequent early symptoms.

Because these initial symptoms are similar to those of many respiratory infections, the health care community will need to be alert to the potential threat and be up-to-date about the symptoms patients exhibit and the appropriate management of patients suspected of having pneumonic plague.

PLAGUE THROUGH THE AGES

There are reports of plaguelike disease in China as early as 224 B.C. In A.D. 541 the first recorded plague epidemic claimed the lives of up to 60 percent of the population of North Africa, Europe, and central and southern Asia.

The second plague epidemic is the one that came to be known as the Black Death. It raged across Europe from 1346 to 1352 and was spread to humans primarily through infected rodents and their fleas. During these six years, the Black Death killed more than one-third of Europe's population, accounting for twenty million to thirty million deaths. The disease moved inexorably from village to village and then was carried by ships as far away as Iceland and Greenland, where the disease may have hastened the demise of the Vikings.

The Black Death took its name from the gruesome appearance of its victims. Some believe the name derived from victims who turned dark purple in their final hours because of respiratory failure. Others say it may have originated from the gangrene that set in on the noses and fingers of some victims toward the end.

The third worldwide epidemic began in China in 1855, spread to every populated continent, and claimed the lives of more than twelve million people in India and China alone.

Pneumonic plague outbreaks have been rare, but extremely deadly. An outbreak in Manchuria in 1910–11 spread the disease to as many as sixty thousand people. A second large outbreak of pneumonic plague occurred there ten years later. In those days before antibiotics, nearly 100 percent of the cases were fatal.

Following these early symptoms, the disease progresses rapidly into pneumonia. If the disease is untreated, death can follow within a day or two. In the days before antibiotics, the time from inhaling the plague bacteria to death was reported to have been just two to six days. In two recent U.S. cases where people contracted

A microscopic view of *Bacillus anthracis*, the bacterium that causes anthrax, shown in its active vegetative state. Note the distinctive rod shape. *Courtesy of Getty Images.*

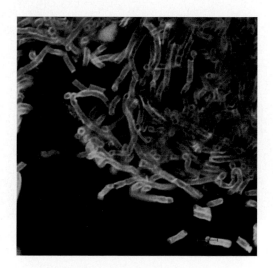

Microscopic view of the anthrax bacterium after it has reproduced. *Courtesy of the Centers for Disease Control and Prevention.*

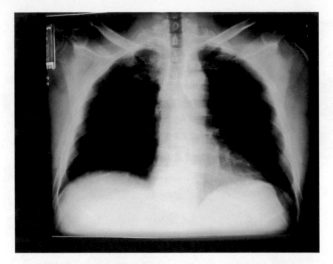

Chest X ray taken of a man in Florida in 2000, one year prior to exposure to anthrax in October 2001. *Courtesy of JFK Medical Center, Atlantis, Florida.*

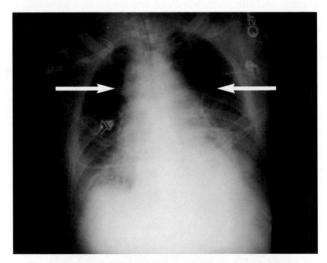

Chest X ray of the same man in Florida after he developed inhalational anthrax in October 2001. The widened area (between arrows) in the middle of the chest, signifying swollen and diseased lymph nodes, is typical of inhalational anthrax. *Courtesy of JFK Medical Center, Atlantis, Florida.*

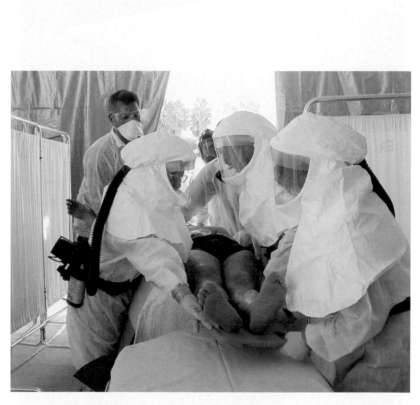

Bioterrorism preparedness drill at JFK Medical Center in Atlantis, Florida, where the first anthrax cases were diagnosed in October 2001. Only one in five hospitals in the United States had developed a bioterrorism preparedness and response plan, according to a 2000 survey. *Courtesy of JFK Medical Center, Atlantis, Florida.*

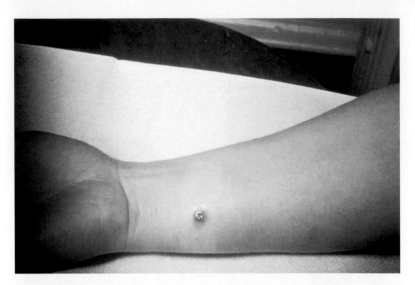

Cutaneous, or skin, anthrax lesion four days after exposure. The lesion is developing into an ulcer, and the arm is swelling. *Courtesy of the Centers for Disease Control and Prevention.*

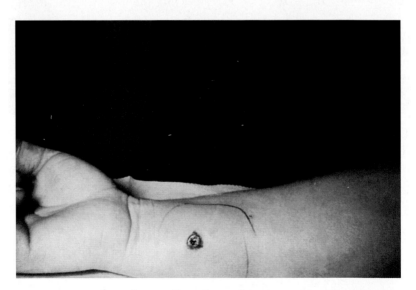

Cutaneous anthrax lesion five days after exposure. The ulcer is enlarged, the base of the ulcer is turning black, and swelling is increased. *Courtesy of the Centers for Disease Control and Prevention.*

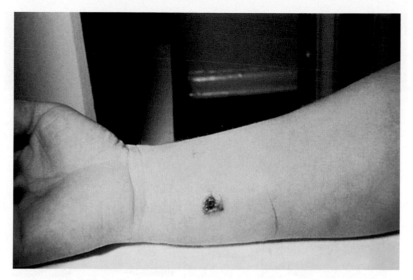

Cutaneous anthrax lesion seven days after exposure. The ulcer base is darker, and the swelling has decreased. *Courtesy of the Centers for Disease Control and Prevention.*

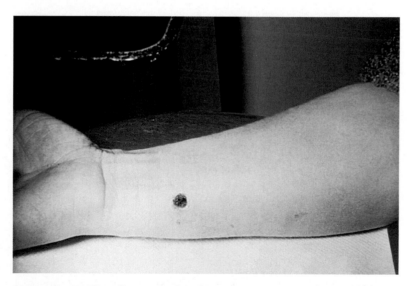

Cutaneous anthrax lesion twelve days after exposure. The lesion is dry and black and will soon separate and fall off. *Courtesy of the Centers for Disease Control and Prevention.*

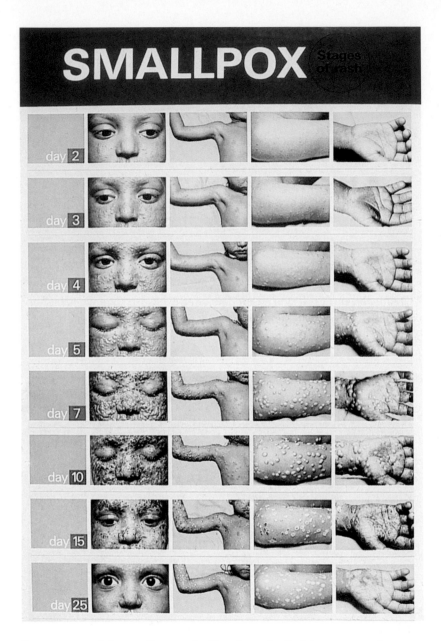

Progression of the smallpox rash. Note how the lesions erupt at the same time. *Courtesy of the World Health Organization,* Smallpox and Its Eradication *(Geneva: WHO, 1988).*

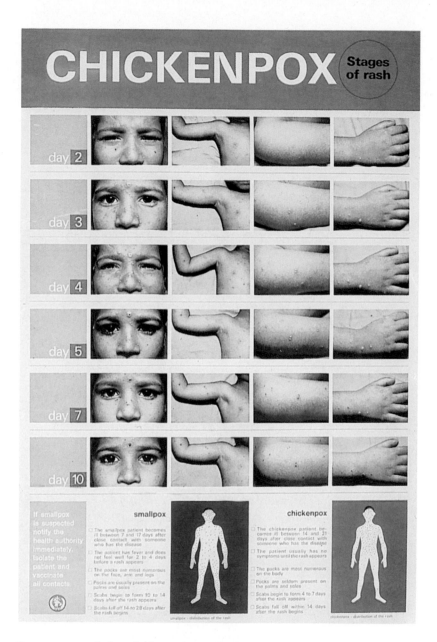

Progression of the chicken pox rash. Note how the lesions are more superficial than smallpox and erupt at different rates. *Courtesy of the World Health Organization,* Smallpox and Its Eradication *(Geneva: WHO, 1988).*

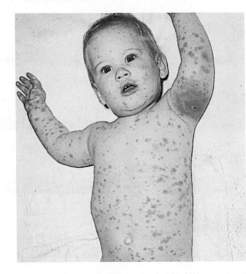

Generalized vaccinia, in which lesions erupt as the vaccine virus is disseminated through the blood, is one of the complications of smallpox vaccination. *Courtesy of the World Health Organization, Smallpox and Its Eradication (Geneva: WHO, 1988).*

Residents of the Rhondda Valley in Wales line up for smallpox vaccinations in 1962, after the World Health Organization confirmed an outbreak in the area. If a smallpox outbreak occurs in the United States, widespread vaccination will be necessary to prevent the disease from spreading. *Courtesy of Getty Images.*

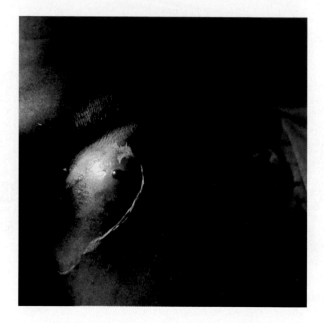

A swollen lymph gland, called a bubo, often appears because of infection from plague bacteria. *Courtesy of David T. Dennis.*

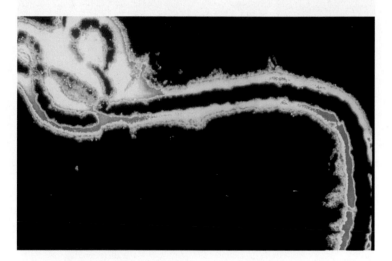

Microscopic view of the Ebola virus—one of two filoviruses, named for their long and stringy, or filamentous, appearance. *Courtesy of Custom Medical Stock.*

Deerflies can carry tularemia and spread the disease to humans.
Courtesy of phototakeusa.

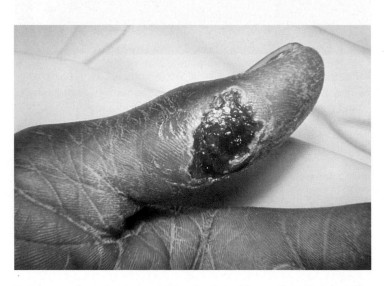

Tularemia skin ulcer, caused by the bite of an infected tick or fly.
Courtesy of the Centers for Disease Control and Prevention.

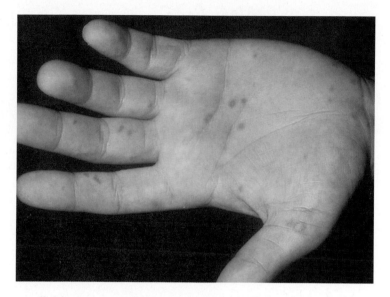

Small blisters on palm and fingers associated with foot-and-mouth disease. *Courtesy of Custom Medical Stock.*

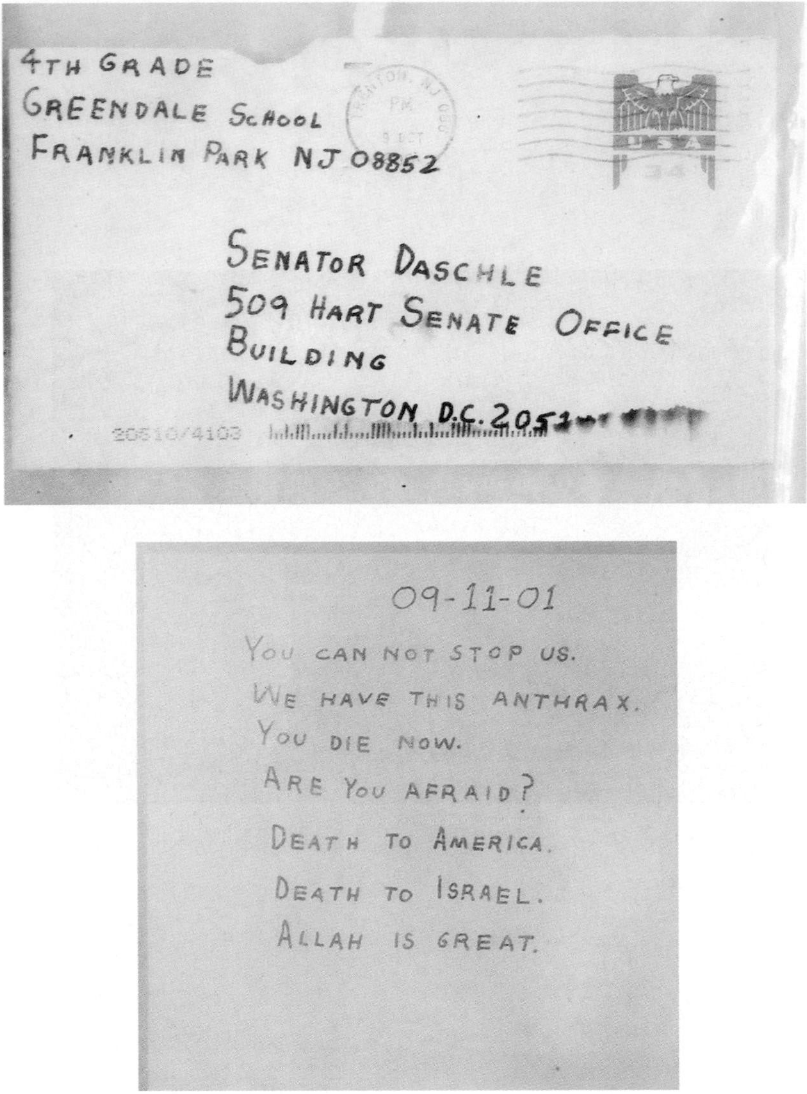

4TH GRADE
GREENDALE School
FRANKLIN PARK NJ 08852

SENATOR DASCHLE
509 HART SENATE OFFICE
BUILDING
WASHINGTON D.C. 2051

09-11-01
YOU CAN NOT STOP US.
WE HAVE THIS ANTHRAX.
YOU DIE NOW.
ARE YOU AFRAID?
DEATH TO AMERICA.
DEATH TO ISRAEL.
ALLAH IS GREAT.

The anthrax-tainted letter sent to Sen. Tom Daschle's Washington, D.C., Hart Senate office on October 15, 2001, began the largest bioterrorism attack on U.S. soil to date. This act of bioterrorism, using a potent form of anthrax, closed the Hart Senate Office Building for three months, while the building was decontaminated. *Courtesy of the Federal Bureau of Investigation.*

While never opened outside the laboratory, this anthrax-laden letter sent to Sen. Patrick Leahy's Washington, D.C., office is believed to have caused significant cross-contamination in the U.S. postal system. Hand-writing and scientific samples from both the Daschle and Leahy letters are being used by the FBI in its criminal investigation of the incident.

Courtesy of the Federal Bureau of Investigation.

A reusable respirator equipped with P100-rated filters. These masks are only effective against certain biological agents if they are prefitted for the individual and are worn at the time of exposure. *Courtesy of Mine Safety Appliances.*

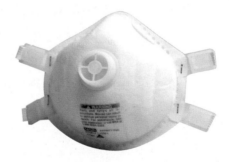

A disposable N95 respirator. An N95 rating indicates that a mask is 95 percent effective at filtering small airborne particles. This disposable mask is appropriate for family disaster supply kits. *Courtesy of Mine Safety Appliances.*

pneumonic plague after handling infected cats, the diagnosis was not made and treatment didn't start until more than twenty-four hours after the first symptoms appeared. Both patients died.

With bubonic plague, it's usually two to eight days before the first symptoms appear: sudden fever, chills, and weakness. Within a few days, the lymph nodes, usually in the groin and armpits, swell and become extremely painful. If the patient doesn't get appropriate care, respiratory failure, shock, and death can follow in two to four days.

Rarely, the bite from an infected flea will lead directly to septicemic plague, in which the bacteria enter the bloodstream, severely damaging organs and causing blood vessels to hemorrhage. Sometimes, gangrene may occur in the nose and fingers, and there may be bleeding from the nose and ears.

Without treatment, septicemic plague is almost always fatal. In the United States over the last fifty years, persons with bubonic or septicemic plague developed pneumonia in about 12 percent of the cases. The last known case of one person spreading plague to another in the United States occurred in Los Angeles in 1924.

DOES PLAGUE STILL EXIST NATURALLY?

The bacterium that causes plague can be found on every populated continent except Australia. Over the last fifty years, an average of 1,700 cases has been reported annually worldwide.

Advances in living conditions, such as control of rodent populations, coupled with the availability of antibiotics make naturally occurring outbreaks of plague far less likely today than in the past. But since animals such as ground squirrels, prairie dogs, and occasionally rabbits and cats may be infected with this bacterium, human infection remains a possibility.

Periodic biological surveys of rodents help public officials assess the likelihood that this infection will emerge in the wild. This information is used to provide the public with guidance regarding the likelihood of contracting plague in specific geographical and ecological settings.

In the United States bubonic plague remains by far the most common form and occurs primarily in the western states of New Mexico, Arizona, Colorado, and California. Of the 390 cases of plague reported in the United States from 1947 to 1996, the vast majority (84 percent) were the bubonic form and only 2 percent developed into pneumonia.

But when pneumonic plague does surface, public concern is heightened. In 1994, the occurrence of a small number of cases of plague in Surat, India, led to panic and fear that an epidemic was about to explode, and approximately half a million people fled the city.

While this fortunately did not develop into a broader outbreak, it highlighted the need for epidemiological and laboratory capacity and expertise to conduct investigations whenever a case of plague occurs. Because of the potential for pneumonic plague to rapidly expand into an epidemic, it's absolutely crucial to quickly determine the source of an outbreak so that appropriate control measures can be implemented.

In addition, the investigation can assess whether the outbreak of plague cases represents a naturally occurring infection or could be the first sign of an intentional release. Information gathered in the course of the investigation is also necessary to keep health care workers, the community, the media, and local and national decision makers updated as part of the effort to manage the evolving public health crisis.

How contagious is plague?

Again, it depends on the form. Pneumonic plague is easily passed from person to person when someone who is infected coughs bacteria into the air. The disease also is considered highly infectious, meaning it is easily contracted from an intentional release of the bacteria into the air.

Bubonic and septicemic plague are spread only through bites from infected fleas, so people who develop this form of the disease are not contagious to others.

Because people who have pneumonic plague are highly contagious, they should be placed in respiratory isolation. Hospital staff should wear respirators—masks that can filter out particles—when they're around patients. Because of the possibility that the disease can be spread to those who come into contact with a pneumonic plague patient, the local and state health departments should be notified immediately.

Reporting a case of plague to local health authorities is required by the World Health Organization's international health regulations so that community monitoring can begin immediately to determine whether the disease is part of a larger outbreak.

In addition, an epidemiological investigation is performed in an attempt to find the source and risk factors of the disease so others can be shielded from exposure. Initial laboratory tests, including a determination of the antibiotics that are likely to be most effective, should be confirmed by a referral laboratory in the state or sent to the Centers for Disease Control and Prevention.

COULD PLAGUE REALLY BE USED AS A WEAPON OF MASS DESTRUCTION?

First, most experts believe this is an unlikely scenario. It would be fairly difficult to obtain the right strain of plague bacteria and even more difficult to process it as a weapon of mass destruction.

But we know that thousands of Soviet scientists in over ten research institutes worked with the bacterium that causes plague. Moreover, they produced hundreds of tons of plague bacteria during the Cold War as a potential bioweapon, so we can't delude ourselves into thinking it can't happen.

In a 1970 analysis, the World Health Organization estimated that if fifty kilograms of plague bacteria were released upwind of a city of 5 million, as many as 150,000 people would develop pneumonic plague, 80,000–100,000 would need to be hospitalized, and 36,000 of those would die. This worst-case scenario depends on a number of factors, including the quantity of bacteria released, the dissemination technique, and meteorological conditions. Once released into the air, the bacteria would remain capable of infecting people for up to one hour, but would then be destroyed by the sun's ultraviolet light. But even if the release were not perfectly executed, the effects of the disease and subsequent social disruption would be substantial.

An interactive bioterrorism preparedness exercise was conducted in Denver in 2000 to gauge how ready top government officials and state and local public health agencies are to respond to a bioterror attack. The drill, called TOPOFF (short for "top officials"), was based on the hypothetical release of plague bacteria at the Denver Performing Arts Center three days before the beginning of the exercise.

It quickly became apparent that the public health system was not ready to handle such an event. It virtually crippled the city and completely overwhelmed hospitals in the first twenty-four hours. There was confusion over who was in charge, how decisions would be made and communicated, how lifesaving antibiotics and simple face masks would be distributed, how hospitals would be supplied and staffed (medical, administrative, and security personnel), and how mandatory quarantine and isolation could be enforced.

By the end of the exercise, there was civil unrest, rioting, and gridlock. It wasn't even clear what the human toll would be. Conflicting reports estimated the number of sick persons at 3,700 to more than 4,000, and the number of dead at 950 to more than 2,000.

This was just a simulation, but it opened our eyes to some of the main challenges we face in dealing with the threat of bioterrorism. Identifying where we need to make improvements was extremely valuable. We found out we were underprepared to deal with such an event. But the drill pointed us in the right direction, especially regarding the need to be able to rapidly increase the number of public health workers available to help control the epidemic without disrupting their other key duties.

Officials at the federal, state, and local levels have already begun addressing these crucial questions. And Sen. Edward M. Kennedy and I joined to write and sponsor (along with more than eighty of our Senate colleagues) the Bioterrorism Preparedness Act of 2001, which is designed to improve our health system's ability to respond to bioterrorism, among other goals. I'll discuss the government's response and the future in the final chapter.

IS THERE A VACCINE AVAILABLE TO PROTECT AGAINST PLAGUE?

No. An old vaccine has been discontinued because of its many side effects. Also, although it helped prevent or ease symptoms of bubonic plague, it was regarded as ineffective against the inhaled form most likely to be used in a bioterror attack.

Work has been under way since the Persian Gulf War on safer, more effective vaccines. That work got a boost last fall when scientists finished decoding the full DNA, or genome, of the bacterium that causes plague. The sample used to decode the genome came from a Colorado veterinarian who died from the inhaled form of the plague—from an infected cat—in 1992. So it's hoped that vaccine researchers will be able to use this new DNA map to develop a vaccine that protects against pneumonic plague.

PLAGUE AS A BIOWEAPON
A Brief History

In Greek mythology, Pandora, the first woman on Earth, was given a box by the gods and told never to open it. Of course, her curiosity got the best of her, and she did, releasing innumerable plagues on an unsuspecting world.

At least Pandora didn't know what she was unleashing. Those who have tried throughout history to use plague as a weapon can't say the same.

The siege of Kaffa in 1346 is widely believed to be the first attempt to use plague as a biological weapon. And a particularly gruesome attempt it was. The invading Tatar forces were struck with a plague epidemic as they set upon the city, which is now Feodosiya, Ukraine. Their leader came up with the idea of turning his forces' misfortune into a tactical advantage by catapulting the corpses of plague victims into the city.

A plague outbreak did indeed erupt in Kaffa, and the Tatars took the city. Retreating forces then carried the plague by ship to Constantinople, Genoa, Venice, and other Mediterranean ports, helping to set off the second plague epidemic in Europe.

Or so the story goes. Given what we know today, it's far from certain that the corpses were responsible for the epidemic. In fact, it's more likely that the plague spread through Kaffa by infected rats and fleas, just as it did through the rest of Europe.

Why? The fleas that carry the disease and spread it to humans feed off living hosts. They pick up the disease from rats and, when the rats die, leave to find another living host, which is often a human. So it's likely the plague-infected fleas would have already left the corpses before they were catapulted over the walls.

Over the years, sadly, the use of plague as a weapon grew more sophisticated—and more deadly. During World War II, a division of the Japanese Imperial Army called Unit 731 tested scores of disease agents, including plague, on Chinese prisoners, killing an estimated ten thousand. The Japanese military also dropped plague-infested fleas from airplanes over populated areas in China, sparking plague outbreaks among civilians.

Following the war, the United States and the Soviets developed techniques to effectively release the plague bacteria into the air, so fleas would no longer be needed. The United States got out of the germ-warfare business in 1969, but the Soviets secretly continued their efforts and produced hundreds of tons of plague bacteria that could be loaded into missiles. Thousands of Soviet scientists reportedly worked with plague during the Cold War years.

The whereabouts of most of those scientists today is unknown, which is a cause for some concern.

Is there an effective treatment for plague?

Yes. The bacterium can be thwarted by a number of antibiotics, but treatment must begin within twenty-four hours after symptoms first appear for the patient to have the best chance of survival. Again, in making the diagnosis and beginning treatment, every moment counts. Streptomycin has historically been the first-choice antibiotic against plague. Administered by injection early in the disease, the drug has cut the death rate to between 5 and 14 percent.

But streptomycin has been infrequently used in the United States, and large stocks are not available. Gentamicin, also administered by injection, is widely available. Physicians have extensive experience using this antibiotic, and it is relatively inexpensive. It has been shown to be at least as effective as streptomycin in treating plague.

Doxycycline and ciprofloxacin (Cipro), which can be taken by mouth, also are effective alternatives. They would be the top choices if a bioterror attack resulted in mass casualties, because they can be dispensed in pill form and could be given to those exposed before the infection was advanced. The logistics of trying to administer shots to large numbers of very ill people would be extremely difficult.

Further complicating matters is the fact that patients with pneumonic plague would require enormous hospital resources. They would have to be isolated for at least the first forty-eight hours, or until their symptoms improved and they were no longer contagious. However, since this type of pneumonia is often very severe, many would require respiratory-support machinery and other support.

In the event of an outbreak of pneumonic plague, it's a good idea for anyone at risk of exposure to wear an N95 respirator, a mask that must be fitted properly to provide maximum protection. For more information on the respirator, see pages 32–36.

6

BOTULISM

ASSESSING THE RISK

Availability HIGH. The toxin is widely available, but the most deadly form is more difficult to obtain. It already has been used unsuccessfully in attempted bioterror attacks by a Japanese cult. Rogue nations Iraq, Iran, North Korea, and Syria are believed to have it.

Stability MEDIUM. It would take considerable technical expertise to stabilize the toxin for aerosol release, and the toxin would lose its effectiveness rapidly because it deteriorates in bright sun. It could be used more easily to contaminate food. But cooking food at 185 degrees Fahrenheit for five minutes destroys the toxin.

Deliverability MEDIUM. It would be hard to weaponize the toxin so it could be released as an aerosol. So it's not very likely to cause mass casualties in this manner. But it could be slipped into uncooked restaurant food such as condiments or a salad bar or placed in a commercial beverage.

Lethality HIGH. Because botulism causes paralysis and respiratory failure, the death rate is extremely high without the use of ventilating machines to support breathing. In cases involving contaminated food, with treatment available the death rate is about 5 percent. But it's expected that rate would be much higher if the toxin were successfully released into the air in a populated area.

The nerve toxin that causes botulism is the most poisonous substance known to science. In theory, just a single gram of botulinum toxin released in aerosol form could kill more than a million people. That has made it one of the most researched and widely developed biological weapons on Earth.

But in an odd medical twist, the toxin can cure as well as kill. It is the first biological toxin to be licensed for treatment of human disease. In the United States it is used to treat two rare eye conditions, blepharospasm and strabismus, both of which involve excessive muscle contractions.

The toxin also is used to help relieve more common conditions, including migraine headache, low back pain, stroke, cerebral palsy, and benign prostate hyperplasia. Under the trade name Botox, it is commonly used by plastic surgeons to remove wrinkles.

WHAT IS BOTULISM?

Botulism is a rare, paralyzing muscle disease that is usually contracted from uncooked or improperly cooked food. Like anthrax, the bacterium *Clostridium botulinum* forms a hard shell, called a spore, to protect itself when the environment turns inhospitable. The spores and bacteria are normally harmless.

It is only when the bacteria grow, releasing the botulinum toxin, that they become dangerous. There are many parallels between the bacteria that cause anthrax and botulism: Both form spores and come naturally from the soil. Neither is transmissible from one person to another, and both can be spread through food and air or enter the body through wounds. And both lead to production of a toxin.

Actually, there are seven distinct types of botulinum toxin, designated by the letters A through G. Only four of them cause illness in humans.

Botulism occurs naturally in three forms: foodborne, infant, and wound. The names pretty much explain each type. On average, 110 cases of botulism are reported in the United States each year.

You can't catch the disease through the skin unless there's a wound, and it doesn't spread from person to person. Although the disease is rare, it is very serious.

WHAT ARE THE SYMPTOMS OF BOTULISM?

Foodborne botulism is the form you're probably most familiar with, although it accounts for only 25 percent of cases in the United States. The toxin enters the body through contaminated food and binds to nerve endings where they join with muscles. It then blocks signals for the muscles to contract, causing paralysis. The first symptoms typically appear within twelve to thirty-six hours after eating contaminated food, although it can be as little as six hours and as long as ten days.

The first symptoms are double vision, blurred vision, drooping eyelids, slurred speech, difficulty swallowing, dry mouth, and muscle weakness. Botulism always begins in the muscles of the head, face, and neck. If untreated, the disease will then work its way down the body, paralyzing the arms, legs, trunk, and respiratory muscles.

The most common form of the disease, accounting for 72 percent of all cases, is infant botulism. In the United States, there are about seventy-five to one hundred cases reported each year. In these cases, normally harmless spores swallowed by an infant will germinate and release the toxin in the large intestine. This form of the disease only strikes babies under one year old and is most common at two months. Symptoms include constipation, lethargy, poor feeding, a weak cry, and poor muscle tone.

Wound botulism is extremely rare; it is usually seen in drug users. The disease acts essentially in the same way as foodborne botulism. Neither infant nor wound botulism is likely to result from a bioterror attack.

HOW OFTEN IS BOTULISM FATAL?

Advances in medicine over the last fifty years have cut the fatality rate for foodborne botulism from about 50 percent to 3 percent. The most common cause of death used to be respiratory failure. But with intensive medical and nursing care, especially the use of ventilators to help them breathe, patients can eventually recover.

However, recovery takes several months because it requires the growth of new motor-nerve endings. So the demands a large number of cases would place on the health care system would be enormous.

For infant botulism, the fatality rate is less than 2 percent, and most infants fully recover with proper treatment. Again, they may have to spend weeks or months on a ventilator.

COULD BOTULINUM TOXIN POISON US THROUGH THE AIR?

Airborne release of the toxin so that it's inhaled by victims has not been studied in humans, but it's thought that the disease would progress in a similar manner to foodborne botulism.

There has not been a successful aerosol release of botulinum toxin, but it's not for lack of trying. In the early 1990s, the Japanese cult Aum Shinrikyo released the toxin into the air in downtown Tokyo and at U.S. military installations in Japan during at least three failed bioterror attempts.

Botulinum toxin is colorless, odorless, and tasteless. It is easy to acquire—the Japanese cult obtained its samples from the soil locally—but difficult to turn into an effective aerosol. It is somewhat reassuring that, even though it was extremely well financed and had access to scientific expertise, Aum Shinrikyo was unable to turn botulinum toxin, or anthrax, into an effective bioweapon. At this point, aerosol delivery remains for the most part theoretical.

COULD TERRORISTS SLIP BOTULINUM TOXIN INTO FOOD?

Using the toxin in food or beverages would be easier. The botulinum toxin is very stable on uncooked foods and untreated beverages. Contamination of a large-volume, ready-to-eat, short-shelf-life product such as a commercial beverage could produce a large number of casualties.

Our water supply is considered safe from this potential bioweapon because the toxin can't survive standard water treatments of chlorination and aeration. Also, the amount needed to poison a reservoir would be enormous, not to mention technically difficult to produce and deliver.

Cooking at temperatures above 185 degrees Fahrenheit for five minutes destroys the toxin, so food that is thoroughly cooked is considered safe. Potential targets for bioterrorists could include salad bars, condiments, and unheated beverages such as beer, wine, soda, and bottled water.

WHAT WOULD BE THE IMPACT OF A BOTULISM ATTACK?

Although the threat is considered small, it must be taken seriously because of the challenges an attack would present to our public health system.

Normally, about 20 percent of patients with foodborne botulism require ventilators and extensive medical support. A large outbreak could quickly overwhelm the number of available ventilators, critical care beds, and skilled personnel. And because recovery is very slow, the demands would continue for months.

Again, fast identification of what's happened is crucial to limiting the impact. And in our fast-moving society, that's a big challenge. Because it may be a few days before symptoms appear, a complete travel and activity history must be taken from any patient who comes down with botulism. A case in Canada clearly shows why.

Over a six-week period, twenty-eight people in two countries contracted botulism after eating an unintentionally contaminated restaurant condiment. All were initially misdiagnosed. Only after a mother and daughter were correctly diagnosed after they returned to their home more than two thousand miles from the restaurant was the botulism link discovered.

BOTULISM AS A BIOWEAPON
A Brief History

The use of botulinum toxin as a biological weapon dates back to World War II. The Japanese biological warfare group, Unit 731, contaminated the food of Chinese prisoners in occupied Manchuria with the toxin, with predictably deadly results.

The United States, fearing that Germany had weaponized botulinum toxin, prepared more than a million doses of vaccine for Allied troops preparing to storm Normandy on D-Day. The United States and the Soviets developed the toxin as a potential weapon during the Cold War, a program that ended in the United States by executive order of President Nixon in 1969.

The Soviets, however, secretly continued to test the toxin as a weapon even after signing the 1972 international treaty banning such research. Soviet scientists even attempted to splice the botulinum toxin gene into other bacteria to create a so-called superbug.

Four countries—Iraq, Iran, North Korea, and Syria—are believed to be developing botulinum toxin as a weapon. All are considered friendly to terrorists. We know that Iraq, leading up to the Gulf War, had loaded the toxin in a hundred bombs and thirteen Scud missile warheads.

After the war, Iraq admitted to a United Nations inspection team that it had produced a staggering nineteen thousand liters of concentrated botulinum toxin—three times more than the amount needed to kill everyone on Earth. Three thousand liters of this stock remain unaccounted for.

As we look to the future, it's unsettling that Iraq viewed botulinum toxin as its main bioweapon of choice.

Although the botulinum toxin is as lethal as any known substance, a terrorist would likely use it to create fear by inflicting a few deaths that would severely destabilize a community. Even if there were no mass casualties, the use of this agent could have a major impact on our society and economy.

IS THERE A VACCINE?

The vaccine that has been in use for thirty years is still considered experimental. It has been used to immunize more than three thousand lab workers in many countries. In the United States, it has been used to protect lab workers who might be exposed to the toxin and to immunize our troops during the Gulf War.

The vaccine is scarce and takes several months to build up immunity. Also, it is very painful to receive, causing considerable swelling in the arm where the injection is given. As rare as the disease is, it wouldn't make sense to vaccinate the entire population.

Strange as it seems, the issue is further complicated by all of the health benefits botulinum toxin offers. Vaccinating everyone against it would deny people the advantages of medications that have been developed or will be in the future.

IS THERE AN EFFECTIVE TREATMENT?

Yes. There is an antitoxin horse serum that is kept by the Centers for Disease Control and Prevention (CDC). Physicians report any botulism cases to the CDC through their state health department. Monitoring cases is essential because if someone contracts botulism from contaminated food, it's possible the poisoned food is still being served and that there could be other cases.

The CDC is ready to ship the botulinum antitoxin anywhere immediately, twenty-four hours a day. The serum blocks the toxin from circulating in the blood. It can stop the disease from worsening, but it cannot reverse any paralysis that has already occurred.

So the sooner it's administered, the better. The serum also can minimize nerve damage.

Depending on how far the disease has advanced, a patient may need to be on a ventilator to aid breathing and may require help with feeding and other support. The paralysis, if treated, will slowly improve, but it will take up to several months.

7

TULAREMIA

ASSESSING THE RISK

Availability MEDIUM. The bacterium occurs naturally in mice, squirrels, and rabbits. It was developed as a bioweapon by Japan, the United States, and the Soviet Union during World War II, and the Soviets reportedly developed antibiotic- and vaccine-resistant strains during the 1980s.

Stability LOW. The bacterium is generally unstable, and it is killed by mild heat and disinfectants. But it can survive for months in cold, moist conditions. If released in aerosol form, it could remain effective in the air for up to two hours if weather conditions are right.

Deliverability MEDIUM. Tularemia bacteria are difficult to process, and even harder to make stable enough to cause mass casualties. But *Francisella tularensis* is one of the most infectious bacteria known, so a successfully engineered attack could infect almost everyone who inhales it.

Lethality MEDIUM TO LOW. With advances in treatment, the death rate in the United States has plunged to less than 2 percent. Left untreated, tularemia pneumonia can kill 30 to 60 percent of the time.

Also known as rabbit fever or deer fly fever, tularemia is a fairly obscure and rare rural disease that made headlines in 2001 when several people on Martha's Vineyard contracted the disease while clearing brush and mowing lawns. It has, however, achieved prominence as a potential biological weapon.

Why? It's one of the most infectious diseases on Earth.

WHAT IS TULAREMIA?

It's a disease caused by the bacterium *Francisella tularensis*. Inhaling as few as ten of the microscopic organisms can trigger the disease, which could lead to serious respiratory illness, including life-threatening pneumonia.

The disease was first recognized in 1911. The number of cases in the United States has dropped dramatically, from several thousand a year in the 1950s to fewer than two hundred annually today. Those most likely to be naturally exposed to tularemia include hunters, trappers, butchers, and farmers. Most natural cases occur in south-central and western states, especially Missouri, Arkansas, Oklahoma, South Dakota, and Montana.

The bacterium that causes the disease is not only highly infectious but also pretty resilient in the right environment. It is found naturally in water, soil, and vegetation in rural areas, and it can survive for months in cold, moist conditions. It also can remain viable for years in frozen rabbit meat.

HOW IS TULAREMIA SPREAD?

In nature, tularemia is primarily an animal disease carried by such small mammals as rabbits, hares, squirrels, voles, mice, and water rats. Humans most often get the disease when they are bitten by infected ticks or, less often, flies, or when bacteria enter through broken skin while they are handling infected animals or carcasses, such as skinning an infected rabbit. Such causes account for 87 percent of natural cases.

Humans also can contract tularemia by eating undercooked,

contaminated food, such as rabbit meat; drinking contaminated water; or inhaling contaminated dust or spray. The disease is not spread from person to person.

WHAT ARE THE SYMPTOMS OF TULAREMIA?

The way the disease attacks the body depends on how it's contracted. The initial symptoms typically appear within three to five days after exposure to the bacteria but can occur from as little as one day to as long as two weeks after exposure. Symptoms include sudden onset of fever, chills, headaches, aches and pains in the muscles and joints—symptoms that are much like the common cold—a dry cough, and progressive weakness.

If the bacteria are inhaled—the method most likely to be used in a bioterror attack—the disease can rapidly progress to pneumonia, with chest pain, difficulty breathing, bloody sputum (a mixture of saliva and mucus), and, if untreated, respiratory failure and death.

In rare cases, the disease can progress to what's called "typhoidal tularemia," which is every bit as deadly as the version with pneumonia. With typhoidal tularemia there may be no X-ray evidence of pneumonia, and the ulcers and swollen lymph nodes that characterize the other most common forms may be absent. Instead, it's a severe blood infection that affects the entire body, and it can result in respiratory and organ failure if not caught in time.

If the disease is contracted from a bite or by handling infected materials, a red spot may appear on the skin at the point of infection and grow into an ulcer. Lymph nodes, particularly in the groin and armpits, become swollen and sore. Those who get the disease by swallowing contaminated food or drink experience inflammation in the throat and painful swelling of the lymph nodes in the neck.

Before antibiotics, up to 15 percent of those with tularemia died, and the death rate soared as high as 60 percent when pneumonia was involved. Now, with antibiotic treatment, fewer than 2 percent in the United States die after infection.

CAN TULAREMIA BE USED AS A BIOLOGICAL WEAPON?

Yes, although it is important to note that it never has been used against people. It has, however, been researched as a bioweapon.

In the 1930s and 1940s, large outbreaks caused by contaminated drinking water erupted in Europe and the Soviet Union. As tularemia demonstrated its natural capacity to cause widespread harm, the Japanese Imperial Army's germ warfare division, Unit 731, began researching tularemia as a potential biological weapon. Some suspect that large outbreaks among Soviet soldiers during World War II were caused by deliberate release of the bacteria, but that has never been proven.

Following World War II, both the United States and the Soviet Union devoted significant resources to developing tularemia as a biological weapon. While the odds of a large-scale bioterror attack with tularemia are fairly remote, the need to be prepared is underscored by a 1970 World Health Organization (WHO) analysis.

The WHO estimated that if fifty kilograms of the bacteria that causes tularemia were released into the air over a metropolitan area of 5 million people, 250,000 would be incapacitated, and 19,000 would die. On the basis of this model, the Centers for Disease Control and Prevention has estimated that the economic toll would also be devastating: $5.4 billion for every 100,000 persons exposed.

IS THERE A VACCINE?

Yes, but today it's only given to lab personnel who routinely work with tularemia bacteria. The vaccine, which is being reviewed by the U.S. Food and Drug Administration, was developed as part of the U.S. military's bioweapons research during the Cold War. It has proven effective against the disease when it's contracted by handling contaminated materials in the laboratory.

However, the vaccine does not fully protect against the inhaled form of the disease. So it wouldn't make sense to vaccinate people in advance, because the inhaled form is the most dangerous and also the most likely to be used in an attack. And it takes fourteen days after vaccination for the protection it does provide to kick in, so the vaccine is not considered for use after people are exposed.

TULAREMIA AS A BIOWEAPON
A Brief History

Tularemia was studied by Japan, the United States, and the Soviet Union during World War II.

Following the war, the U.S. and Soviet military developed and stockpiled weapons that would release tularemia bacteria in aerosol form. Under its biological warfare program, the United States also created vaccines and antibiotic treatments to protect against the bioweapon threat.

After the United States destroyed its stockpile of biological weapons in the early 1970s, the Soviets continued to work with tularemia and other potential biological agents. It has been reported that the Soviets even engineered strains of the tularemia bacterium that are resistant to antibiotics and vaccines.

IS THERE AN EFFECTIVE TREATMENT?

Yes. Antibiotics, started early, are very effective. Streptomycin is the first choice, and gentamicin is an acceptable alternative. Both would be given by injection, and treatment would continue for ten days. Doxycycline and ciprofloxacin (Cipro) are also effective. If doxycycline is used, it is continued for fourteen days to reduce the chance of relapse. Ciprofloxacin is given for ten days. Children would receive the same medications, but at smaller doses. Gentamicin is the top choice for pregnant women.

If a large-scale attack resulted in mass casualties, the first choices would be doxycycline and ciprofloxacin, taken orally, for both adults and children. The reason: It's far more efficient to dispense pills than to give large numbers of injections. Both would be available within hours through the National Pharmaceutical Stockpile program to supplement local needs. If there were a mass casualty, ciprofloxacin would be the drug of first choice for pregnant women.

HOW WOULD WE BE ABLE TO TELL IF TULAREMIA WAS USED AS A BIOLOGICAL WEAPON?

It could be hard to distinguish tularemia from other possible causes of fever. Initially, as people start showing up with respiratory problems, it could be mistaken for influenza (the flu) or pneumonia. The tip-off would be when large numbers of previously healthy adults and children quickly become seriously ill. Even then, it would take some detective work to identify tularemia, as opposed to inhalational plague or anthrax. Plague would progress to severe pneumonia more rapidly than tularemia. And anthrax could be distinguished by the characteristic X ray showing a swelling of the lymph nodes between the lungs, in the part of the chest known as the mediastinum.

There are tests of blood, sputum, biopsy specimens, and other fluid samples to confirm tularemia. But these tests take time, and they can only be conducted at a few labs equipped to handle the highly infectious bacteria. There is no quick diagnostic test to confirm tularemia, so it will be important for public health officials to make the right call based on the symptoms they see. Early identification, rapid communication, and efficient coordination among all parts of the health care system will be crucial.

Confirmation of a tularemia outbreak in a metropolitan area is almost a sure sign that the bacteria were deliberately released, since all previous outbreaks of the disease have occurred in rural areas.

8

EBOLA AND OTHER VIRAL HEMORRHAGIC FEVERS

ASSESSING THE RISK

Availability MEDIUM. It would be very difficult to obtain a strain of Ebola, but it would be easier to obtain strains of arenaviruses from rodents in their natural habitat.

Stability LOW. The viruses are generally unstable, although it has been demonstrated that some can be produced in aerosol form.

Deliverability LOW. These viruses are highly infectious, and there's a lot that science doesn't know about them, especially Ebola. The technology required to produce VHFs, provided the right strain could be obtained, is not considered to be highly advanced. But it would be extremely dangerous and difficult for anyone to weaponize one of the viruses.

Lethality VERY HIGH. This is the biggest concern. Ebola kills up to 90 percent of those infected, depending on the strain, and there is no treatment or vaccine.

One of the things that makes the Ebola virus so frightening is how little we actually know about it. We don't know, for instance, where the disease originated or even how it is naturally spread.

What we do know is that it kills with frightening efficiency—up to 90 percent of its victims die. And we know that, along with the other diseases known as viral hemorrhagic fevers, it is a bioterror threat we cannot ignore.

WHAT ARE VIRAL HEMORRHAGIC FEVERS?

Hemorrhagic fever can result from infection by one of several viruses. The best-known of these viruses is the Ebola virus, named for the river valley in Zaire (now the Democratic Republic of Congo) where the first outbreak occurred in the mid-1970s.

The name viral hemorrhagic fever (VHF) actually tells you a lot about this illness. These infections cause high fever and wide-spread, uncontrollable bleeding. The term "hemorrhagic" refers to one of the disease's most gory and frightful characteristics: In its most severe form, infection causes bleeding under the skin, in internal organs, and from the mouth, nose, ears, eyes, or other body openings.

It's important to note up front that humans are not natural carriers, or hosts, for the organisms that cause VHFs. These viruses normally rely on animals or insects as disease carriers. But once an outbreak begins, the virus can be spread from person to person through direct contact with blood or body fluids.

Of the four viral families that cause VHFs, we're only going to concern ourselves with the two that are considered most likely to be used by bioterrorists. They are the filoviruses, which include Ebola and Marburg hemorrhagic fevers, and the arenaviruses, which include Lassa and South American hemorrhagic fevers.

WHAT ARE FILOVIRUSES?

When examined in a microscope, filoviruses appear long and stringy, or filamentous, and so they were named for their distinctive appearance.

The first virus was discovered during a fatal outbreak that occurred in 1967, when laboratory workers in Marburg, Germany, and Belgrade, Yugoslavia, developed hemorrhagic fever after handling tissues from African green monkeys that had been imported for research. The outbreak resulted in thirty-one cases and seven deaths. The specific virus was named after Marburg, and it disappeared as mysteriously as it first surfaced. Then, in 1975, a traveler who likely was exposed to the virus in Zimbabwe became ill in South Africa, passing the virus along to his traveling companion and a nurse.

In 1976, Ebola became the second and, to date, the only other member admitted to the filovirus family. But, believe me, those two are more than enough. Ebola, which comes in four different strains, was first identified when outbreaks of VHF occurred in northern Zaire and southern Sudan. It proved even more deadly than its Marburg cousin. It killed 90 percent of the people in the Zaire outbreak, and half of those infected in Sudan.

Scientists discovered that the two outbreaks were actually caused by two different, but related, strains of the virus; they came to be named Ebola–Zaire and Ebola–Sudan.

A third strain was identified in the United States in 1989, when hemorrhagic fever swept through Asiatic monkeys that had been imported for research to a Reston, Virginia, primate quarantine facility. Fortunately, this particular strain, named Ebola–Reston, did not cause illness in lab workers who were infected.

Although there were no human casualties, the outbreak, occurring as it did near our nation's capital, brought Ebola to national consciousness. Its fame was further enhanced after it was chronicled in

Richard Preston's best-selling book, *The Hot Zone*.

The fourth strain, Ebola–Ivory Coast, was identified in a patient in the Ivory Coast in 1994. This was the first time the disease had been discovered in West Africa.

Since 1976, Ebola outbreaks have occurred sporadically in Africa. A 1995 outbreak in Kikwit, Zaire, claimed the lives of 80 percent of the 316 people known to have contracted the disease. Unfortunately, natural Ebola virus outbreaks have continued into the twenty-first century. An extended outbreak in the Gulu district of Uganda occurred in the fall of 2000, and another claimed the lives of dozens in west-central Africa in 2001. These outbreaks are a grim reminder that we have yet to understand where this virus hides when it is not infecting people and that it remains an ongoing threat, especially in certain parts of central Africa.

HOW ARE EBOLA AND MARBURG HEMORRHAGIC FEVERS SPREAD?

On the basis of what we know from outbreaks of similar diseases, we suspect that Ebola and Marburg hemorrhagic fevers are carried by animals native to Africa and the Philippines (source of the Ebola–Reston strain). And there is some evidence that certain bats native to the area where the virus has been found may be carriers, but we don't really know for sure.

Because we don't know which animals are the natural hosts for the filoviruses, we don't know with certainty how humans are infected at the start of an outbreak. We also don't know how to interrupt the chain of infection in nature, for example, as we do for West Nile virus, where we can reduce the spread to humans by spraying mosquitoes. However, we suspect that the first patient gets the disease from contact with an infected animal.

Once a person has been infected, we know how the disease spreads to others: by direct body contact with infected blood or body fluids, such as sweat, saliva, or semen. That's why the out-breaks we've seen in Africa have usually spread through family members and friends first. Contaminated needles or syringes also can spread the disease.

The concern among U.S. intelligence, military, and health experts is that VHF could be released in aerosol form. The Soviets, we now know, made aerosolizing Ebola a high priority in their secret bioweapons program. There even are reports that the weaponized strain they developed was named after a scientist who died of the disease.

VHF AS A BIOWEAPON
A Brief History

We know that the Soviet Union, as part of its extensive Cold War bioweapons pro-gram, devoted a high priority to developing the Ebola virus as a weapon of mass destruc-tion. Ken Alibek, a former senior scientist in the Soviet bioweapons program who defected to the United States in 1992, has stated that they even conducted experiments attempt-ing to blend Ebola with smallpox.

More recently, members of the Aum Shinrikyo cult in Japan traveled to Zaire in 1992 to try to obtain Ebola virus as part of their bioterror campaign. They were unsuccessful.

Although Ebola has never spread person-to-person on U.S. soil, we have experienced firsthand the horror of hemorrhagic fever. A yellow fever outbreak in 1793 in Philadelphia, then the nation's capital, claimed the lives of 10 percent of the city's population and caused widespread panic.

Many of these viruses are naturally infectious as small particles in the laboratory. That is why they are researched only in labs that meet the most stringent biosafety standards, level 4. As we discov-ered in the Reston case, airborne viruses can easily infect animals, although we have not seen this happen in humans.

While some strains of virus, such as yellow fever, are quite sta-ble in aerosol form, the filoviruses are not considered particularly stable. However, the Soviets experimented with various additives to increase the stability of the Marburg virus.

Obtaining the virus to make an aerosol would be extremely difficult, and it is thought to be beyond the capabilities of terrorist groups. And handling the virus would be extremely dangerous for anyone attempting to weaponize it.

WHAT ARE THE SYMPTOMS OF EBOLA?

The incubation period, or time between exposure to the virus and the first symptoms, can be as short as several days or as long as three weeks. The first symptoms for most Ebola patients include high fever, headache, muscle aches, stomach pain, fatigue, and diarrhea. Some also experience sore throat, hiccups, skin rash, red and itchy eyes, blood in vomit, and bloody diarrhea.

Within a week after the first symptoms appear, the disease can progress to chest pain, shock, and even death. The fatality rate for the disease usually ranges from 50 to 90 percent, depending on the particular strain involved. Another thing we don't know about Ebola is why some people are able to recover while others aren't.

WHAT ARE THE SYMPTOMS OF MARBURG?

After a five-to-ten-day incubation period, symptoms come on with a rush: high fever, chills, headache, and fatigue. About five days later, a red raised skin rash extending over a large area often appears, usually on the chest, back, and stomach. It's followed by nausea, vomiting, chest pain, sore throat, stomach pain, and diarrhea. The symptoms continue to grow more severe and may include jaundice, inflammation of the pancreas, severe weight loss, confusion, shock, liver failure and other internal organ problems, and the characteristic massive bleeding. About one in four people with the disease dies, although there have been outbreaks where as many as three in four die.

IS THERE A TREATMENT OR VACCINE FOR EBOLA OR MARBURG?

No. The best that can be done is to support patients in the hospital by balancing their fluids and electrolytes, maintaining their oxygen levels and blood pressure, giving blood transfusions, and treating them for complicating infections.

IF THERE WERE AN OUTBREAK OF VHF, WHAT COULD WE DO?

In many of the outbreaks in Africa, the disease has spread quickly through hospitals because health care workers treating patients often don't wear masks, gowns, or gloves. Also, reuse of contaminated needles and syringes can spread the disease.

Isolating patients and taking necessary precautions with protective clothing and face masks, hand washing, and other barriers to spreading the virus can help contain the disease. Education is also crucial. People must be taught to prevent the disease by avoiding direct body contact with body fluids or contaminated clothing or bedding. This could reduce the spread among family members and friends.

IS THE USE OF EBOLA OR OTHER VHFS AS A BIOWEAPON REALLY A POSSIBILITY?

There has never been a case of the Ebola VHF in humans in the United States. But it certainly belongs on the CDC's list of highest-priority bioterror agents.

- It could potentially be highly infectious in aerosol form.

- It causes severe illness and has a high fatality rate.

- There is no treatment or vaccine.

- An outbreak is likely to cause panic.

- The Soviets made it a high priority in their clandestine offensive bioweapons program during the Cold War.

Given those factors, we have no choice but to consider Ebola a potential bioweapon.

WHAT ARE ARENAVIRUSES?

The arenaviruses are a much larger family than the filoviruses, and their natural hosts are known: rodents. This category of viruses was first discovered in 1933, but the first member known to cause viral hemorrhagic fever, the Junin virus, was identified in 1958. Junin caused Argentine hemorrhagic fever in a large agricultural area in Argentina.

Other arenaviruses associated with VHF are Machupo, isolated in 1963 in Bolivia; Lassa, identified in West Africa in 1969; and the two most recent additions, Guanarito, discovered in Venezuela, and Sabia, found in Brazil. Junin, Machupo, Guanarito, and Sabia are collectively known as South American VHFs.

HOW ARE ARENAVIRUSES SPREAD?

Once again, we know a lot more about arenaviruses than we do about filoviruses. The arenaviruses are passed from generation to generation through the rodents that carry them. However, the virus doesn't appear to cause illness in the host rats and mice.

As with Ebola virus infections, humans are not a natural host for Lassa or the South American viruses. Humans contract the disease by direct contact with infected rodents or their urine or droppings. This can happen in various ways, including eating contaminated food, coming in contact with rodent excrement through broken skin, or inhaling tiny particles contaminated by rodent urine or excrement.

Once a person is infected, the disease can spread to others in the same way as Ebola and Marburg: through direct contact with infected blood or body fluids, and through contaminated medical equipment, such as needles and syringes. Unlike Ebola, though, there have been reports of airborne transmission of two of the arenaviruses, so wearing protective clothing, especially an N95 respirator mask, is essential when around infected patients or patients suspected of having the infection.

WHAT ARE THE SYMPTOMS OF THE LASSA AND SOUTH AMERICAN VHFs?

The incubation period between exposure to the virus and the first symptoms ranges from one to three weeks. In general, Lassa fever is not as severe as the others. Only about 20 percent of those infected with the Lassa strain develop severe illness. The rest come down with only a mild case or show no signs of illness at all.

For those who get the severe disease, symptoms are similar to Ebola and Marburg. In addition, Lassa fever often involves hearing loss, tremors, and inflammation of the brain, or encephalitis, as well as serious breathing problems.

Overall, the disease kills less than 1 percent of those infected. However, among those who get the severe version, the death rate is as high as 20 percent. Pregnant women are most at risk for the severe disease.

South American hemorrhagic fevers are remarkably similar. Between one and two weeks after exposure to the virus, patients gradually experience fever, malaise, severe loss of appetite (anorexia), and fatigue. Those symptoms are soon followed by headache, back pain, dizziness, and stomach problems.

Flushing of the face and chest, tiny hemorrhages in the skin, redness of the eyes, and shock then occur. Within a week to ten days, most patients begin to improve and go on to a full recovery.

But in about 30 percent of cases, the disease progress along one of three more severe paths:

- Pronounced bleeding from body openings, along with widespread bruising

- Delirium, coma, and seizures

- A mixture of bleeding and neurological symptoms

Without treatment, 20 to 30 percent of those with South American hemorrhagic fevers die.

IS THERE A TREATMENT OR VACCINE FOR LASSA AND SOUTH AMERICAN VHFS?

Again, we're ahead of where we are with Ebola and Marburg. An antiviral drug called ribavirin has been successful treating Lassa fever, especially if it's used early in the illness. However, the drug isn't approved in the United States for use against VHFs. And there is no vaccine.

For Junin, considered the main bioterror threat among the arenaviruses, an immune serum has been used to treat some cases. Ribavirin also should be effective, but, again, it isn't approved for this use in the United States. Likewise, a vaccine has been developed for Junin, but it also is not approved in the United States.

As with Ebola and Marburg, the staples of treatment include maintaining fluids and electrolytes and carefully monitoring blood pressure.

If there were an outbreak, the same precautions would need to be taken as with Ebola and Marburg: isolating patients; wearing masks, gowns, and gloves when near someone who is infected; and making sure equipment such as needles and syringes are kept sterile.

9

CHEMICAL WEAPONS

First, let me say that although this book deals primarily with the threats of biological terrorism and what we need to do to be prepared, I've received a lot of questions about chemical weapons. Although biological and chemical weapons are two separate and distinct categories, I think many in the public understandably lump them together. And the fact that hostile nations as well as known terrorist groups have sought to develop both underscores the need to offer at least a quick overview of the most important issues we face with chemical weapons.

In assessing the relative threat posed by biological and chemical weapons, it appears there is a trade-off. Chemical weapons, in general, are not as likely to cause mass casualties or death as biological weapons. But chemical weapons, again speaking generally, tend to be easier to make and use.

The Aum Shinrikyo case in Japan is instructive here. The Japanese doomsday cult had money—they spent an estimated $30 million on their chemical and biological terror program—and recruited scientists and graduate students with considerable technical expertise.

In the early 1990s, they tried on several occasions to release biological agents—anthrax and botulism—in Tokyo and near U.S. military installations in Japan. Each attempt failed.

Finally, in 1995, cult members filled plastic bags with the chemical agent Sarin, brought them to five different locations in the Tokyo subway system, and poked holes in the bags with umbrellas. As a result of these attacks, twelve people died, a thousand were hospitalized, and thirty-eight hundred were injured.

In no way do I want to minimize the horrible pain and suffering those victimized by this cowardly attack endured. But for all of the cult's money, technical skill, and persistence, its members fell far short of their goal of causing widespread death.

This gives us some perspective on the potential threat. Not that we should grow complacent, but we should recognize how difficult it is for even a well-organized, well-funded organization to plan and carry out a successful attack.

Sarin is one of a class of chemical weapons known as nerve agents. These, along with the group known as blister agents, are the two categories most often viewed as potential terrorist threats.

WHAT IS THE DIFFERENCE BETWEEN A CHEMICAL AND A BIOLOGICAL ATTACK?

Both can be dispersed in the air we breathe, the water we drink, and on surfaces we routinely touch.

Signs that a chemical attack has occurred would be expected to appear within minutes to hours. The first indications frequently are things we can see or smell, such as dead insects and animals, colored residues, or distinctive odors.

A biological attack may not make itself known for days to weeks, and there typically are no obvious environmental signatures, such as dead birds falling out of the sky. This delay allows people who have been infected to travel great distances before any medical symptoms appear. That could make it difficult to pinpoint where and when the attack took place.

HOW WOULD I KNOW IF A CHEMICAL ATTACK HAS OCCURRED?

Observe the surroundings. The signs around you will likely tell much of the story. Look out for large numbers of dead animals, birds, or fish in the same area. Note if there is a lack of insect life that you might normally expect.

What about others around you? In a chemical attack, there could be numerous people breaking out in unexplained watery blisters, choking, exhibiting dilating pupils, or experiencing breathing problems. There could be a lot of people with unexplained rashes, nausea, or disorientation. And more than one person suddenly going into convulsions is a clear giveaway.

Be suspicious if you notice numerous surfaces with oily droplets or a film, or if you see numerous surfaces of water with an oily film.

With odors, the key is to notice if the odor you smell is simply out of character for the environment you are in. For example, mustard gas smells like rotten onions.

WHAT ARE NERVE AGENTS, AND HOW DO THEY WORK?

As the name implies, these chemicals work on the nervous system. Colorless and odorless in their pure state, nerve agents are extremely toxic. And they can work with frightening speed, especially if they're inhaled, as was the case in the Tokyo attack.

Nerve agents are liquid at room temperature, but also can be produced as gases or aerosols. They enter the body either through inhalation or through the skin. It's also possible to contaminate food or liquids with nerve agents.

They work by disrupting the transmission of nerve impulses within the nervous system. The nerve agent destroys an essential enzyme that acts as a messenger to let your glands and voluntary muscles know when they've been stimulated enough. When this messenger enzyme is killed, the glands and muscles continue to be stimulated uncontrollably.

The two nerve agents considered most likely to be used by terrorists are Sarin and Tabun. Tabun, originally developed as an insecticide by German chemists in the 1930s, was the very first nerve agent.

WHAT ARE THE SYMPTOMS OF A NERVE AGENT ATTACK?

It depends on how the chemical enters the body. It works very rapidly when inhaled, because the nerve agent immediately gets into the bloodstream through the blood vessels in the lungs and heads straight for the target organs.

Depending on the dose a person has been exposed to, symptoms can show up anywhere from a few minutes to one hour after the attack. The symptoms include watery eyes, runny nose, chest tightness, nausea, and vomiting. Persons exposed to a relatively high dose may experience coughing, difficulty breathing, drooling and excessive sweating, blurred vision, stomach cramps, loss of bladder and bowel control, and twitching, jerking, staggering, or convulsions.

If exposed to a high dose, the victim may quickly go into convulsions, lose consciousness, and die of suffocation because the muscles tire and can no longer sustain breathing functions. This can happen within a matter of minutes.

Exposure to nerve agents is diagnosed from the symptoms. There is no specific diagnostic test.

IS THERE A TREATMENT FOR NERVE AGENTS?

There is no antidote or vaccine. As a general rule, if you see one person on the ground choking or in convulsions, it likely is just a heart attack or seizure. But if you see several people fall to the ground choking and convulsing, assume there has been a chemical attack and immediately leave the area and dial 911. Tell the dispatcher that a hazardous gas may have been released. (For more information on what to tell the dispatcher, see pages 27–28.)

As quickly as possible, take off your clothes, place them in a plastic bag, and seal it. If your clothes are contaminated, they can spread the substance to others. Wash your skin thoroughly and aggressively with soap and water. If only water is available, wash off with water. Try to remain calm. Even if you show no signs of illness, you should be checked by a paramedic or physician responding to the scene.

If you are ill, you'll likely receive an injection of atropine, pralidoxime chloride, or diazepam to ease symptoms.

WHAT ARE BLISTER AGENTS?

Again, the name is fairly descriptive. These chemical weapons cause wounds that resemble burns or blisters. What the name doesn't tell us is that these chemicals damage the respiratory tract when inhaled. The two blister agents most widely viewed as potential terrorist threats are mustard and Lewisite.

You may have heard mustard agent referred to as mustard gas. Actually, it's liquid at room temperature, but it can also be released in the form of a gas.

Mustard agent has a long history of use as a chemical weapon. The German military used it extensively in World War I, leaving many soldiers with permanent eye injuries and chronic respiratory illnesses. But fewer than 3 percent of U.S. mustard casualties died. It was used again in World War II, and it reportedly was used by Iraq in its war against Iran in the 1980s. Up to a thousand Iranian deaths have been attributed to mustard agent.

There are several varieties of mustard agent, including sulfur mustard. It's relatively simple to manufacture, but any large purchase of the precursor chemicals needed to make it would likely be detected.

As a weapon of mass destruction, mustard agent has a limited usefulness. It is more effective at incapacitating people than killing them on a large scale.

The same is true of Lewisite, which can be produced in liquid or vapor form.

WHAT ARE THE SYMPTOMS OF BLISTER AGENTS?

It depends on the agent. Mustard often has a delayed reaction, and it may be hours before you realize you were exposed. Lewisite, on the other hand, causes an immediate, painful reaction.

Mustard agents are colorless and almost odorless, although it's said that mustard can give off a smell similar to rotten onions. However, the chemicals can damage the respiratory system in concentrations so low that they couldn't even be detected by the sense of smell.

Mustard agents typically attack the skin, eyes, lungs, and gastrointestinal tract. They may also eventually damage blood-generating organs as the agent is circulated through the body.

Reaction to a mustard attack is usually delayed, unless a high dose is involved. Once someone is exposed to mustard agent, it can take from two to twenty-four hours before symptoms appear. A mild case may cause aching, tearing eyes, red, irritated skin, hoarseness, coughing, and sneezing.

More severe exposure may cause small blisters that, over several hours, gradually combine to form large blisters. Nausea, vomiting, diarrhea, fever, loss of eyesight, and severe respiratory problems also can occur in serious cases of mustard exposure.

Exposure to Lewisite causes an immediate burning or pain in the eyes, nose, and skin. To make matters worse, fresh air increases the pain. Within minutes, skin can turn grayish owing to tissue damage. Later, severe damage to the eyes, skin, and airways may occur.

IS THERE A TREATMENT FOR BLISTER AGENTS?

There is no vaccine for mustard or Lewisite, and there is no antidote for mustard agents. However, there is an antidote for Lewisite, known as British anti-Lewisite.

For any attack involving a blister agent, immediately remove all clothing, place it in a plastic bag, and seal it. Mustard and Lewisite are considered "persistent" in the environment, which means they won't evaporate within twenty-four hours under normal conditions. That greatly increases the chances of harming others by exposure to contaminated clothing.

If you've been exposed to mustard, flush your skin with water, then wash thoroughly with soap and water. There is a urine test to confirm if you've been exposed to mustard.

If you were exposed to Lewisite, flush your skin with a very diluted amount of household bleach, then wash thoroughly with soap and water. There is no specific diagnostic test for Lewisite.

Recovery from blister agents is slow, but even extensive skin damage can be cured. The key is to keep the patient free of infection. Constant medical care and plastic surgery may be necessary over several months.

**ARE THERE ANY OTHER CHEMICAL WEAPONS WE SHOULD BE
CONCERNED ABOUT?**

Hydrogen cyanide is of great concern because it's so easy to make.
All it takes is mixing a cyanide salt, such as potassium cyanide, with
a strong acid. These materials are readily available and can be pur-
chased in quantity. In fact, these chemicals and a device to mix
them were found in Tokyo subway restrooms a few weeks after the
Sarin nerve agent attack.

Hydrogen cyanide is a liquid that evaporates very quickly, causing vapors or gas to rise. Because these vapors are lighter than air,
hydrogen cyanide is unlikely to be used outdoors. But it could be
very effective indoors.

In small amounts, hydrogen cyanide would have no effect. In
medium doses, it would cause dizziness, nausea, and weakness. In
large amounts, it is extremely toxic, potentially causing loss of
consciousness, convulsions, stopped breathing, and death within
minutes.

In a famous case, hydrogen cyanide was spiked into Tylenol in
the United States in 1982 and caused considerable panic. It also
resulted in the development of tamper-resistant packaging to help
prevent other such incidents.

10

THE THREAT TO OUR FOOD AND WATER SUPPLY

One of the most frequent questions people have asked me since the September 11 attacks regards the safety of our food supply. U.S. Health and Human Services Secretary Tommy G. Thompson spoke for many when, in testimony before Congress, he candidly admitted, "I am more fearful about this than anything else."

Almost a thousand people are hospitalized each and every day in our country due to foodborne diseases. More than five thousand people die each year from such illnesses. This high fatality rate coupled with the ease with which a terrorist could obtain a harmful organism (such as the ever present salmonella or *E. coli*) leads many to believe that as we consider bioterrorism, we are most vulnerable in our food supply. Indeed, the most notable bioterrorist attack on U.S. soil prior to the anthrax events of last year was the intentional food poisoning of 751 people in 1984 (see sidebar, page 141).

Our water supply is generally considered safe, but there still is some anxiety over the threat of bioterrorism. That threat even reaches to our farms and has given rise to another term I wish we never had to learn: agroterrorism.

HOW SAFE IS OUR FOOD?

Generally, our food supply is among the safest on Earth. High standards are consistently maintained. But we recognize that our food is particularly vulnerable to a potential biological attack, primarily because of inadequate governmental oversight.

The Food and Drug Administration (FDA) presently has fewer than 800 food inspectors to oversee food imports at more than 300 ports of entry and to inspect 57,000 sites across the country. It's an impossible task for so few inspectors. Furthermore, the FDA inspects many food manufacturers only once every eight to ten years, and only 1 percent of all food imports are properly inspected. This leaves our food supply highly vulnerable to the determined terrorist.

Three of the "major" biochemical agents that are on the list of most likely offenders in the hands of a terrorist—anthrax, tularemia, and botulinum toxin—may be transmitted through the food supply. And other agents, such as salmonella and *E. coli,* are also easily transmitted in that manner. So we should be doing more to inspect and protect our imported and domestic food supply. In this new age of bioterrorism, we can no longer take for granted the safety of our food supply.

WHO'S IN CHARGE OF FOOD SAFETY?

It can get confusing. The U.S. Department of Agriculture (USDA) and the FDA have different, but sometimes overlapping, areas of responsibility. The FDA is responsible for overseeing any food that is already on the market that may be adulterated or misbranded. The USDA is responsible for inspecting all meat, poultry, and egg products before they reach the market.

The USDA, through the Food Safety Inspection Service (FSIS), has more than 7,500 inspectors who are required by law to be continuously present when processing is going on at any of the nation's 6,000 meat and poultry plants.

The FDA, with between 700 and 800 inspectors, conducts about 13,000 inspections per year. Owing to inadequate resources, inspectors can only get to about 7,000 of the more than 57,000 warehouses, wholesalers, and processors under the agency's jurisdiction. The FDA also inspects about 1,700 juice processors annually.

That means the agency is only inspecting roughly 12 percent of its areas of responsibility each year. Furthermore, the FDA is supposed to inspect high-risk foods (seafood, canned foods, and prepared foods) twice a year, medium-risk foods every two years, and low-risk foods every three years. You should know that these golals are not being met. And this is the food you and your family eat every day.

The FDA's inspection team includes only 175 food importation inspectors for the more than 300 ports of entry nationwide. The FDA views and inspects all food importation paperwork. However, inspectors actually sample and test only 1 percent of all food imports—a figure the FDA would like to increase to 5 percent. There are more than 4 million shipments of food imports per year.

WHAT FOODBORNE DISEASES ARE POTENTIAL BIOTERROR THREATS?

More than two hundred known diseases are spread through food. Each year, foodborne diseases cause 5,000 deaths, hospitalize 325,000 people, and cause 76 million illnesses.

Terrorists would be expected to choose diseases with the highest fatality rates. These include botulism, brucellosis, listeriosis, and *Vibrio vulnificus*. (For detailed information on botulism, see chapter 6.)

Here's a quick overview of the other diseases.

Brucellosis

This infectious disease is caused by the bacterium *Brucella*. The most common way people get the disease is by eating or drinking contaminated milk products. It also can be contracted by direct contact with infected animals or animal products.

Symptoms of brucellosis include fever, sweats, headache, back pain, and weakness. In some cases, severe infections of the central nervous system or lining of the heart may occur. Brucellosis also can cause long-lasting or chronic symptoms that include recurring fevers, joint pain, and fatigue.

More than half—55 percent—of those with brucellosis require hospitalization, but the fatality rate is relatively low, at 5 percent. A combination of the antibiotics doxycycline and rifampin is usually prescribed for six weeks to prevent recurring illness. Depending on when treatment starts and the severity of the illness, recovery may take a few weeks to several months.

Listeriosis

Eating food contaminated with the bacterium *Listeria monocytogenes* causes this very serious disease. Symptoms include fever, muscle aches, and gastrointestinal problems such as nausea and diarrhea.

If the infection spreads to the nervous system, symptoms such as headache, stiff neck, confusion, loss of balance, or convulsions may occur.

Pregnant women who contract listeriosis may only experience a

BIOTERRORISM AT THE SALAD BAR

For the United States, a bioterrorist attack on our food supply is not merely hypothetical. It has already happened here.

In September 1984 an outbreak of food poisoning caused by the bacterium *Salmonella typhimurium* swept through the community of The Dalles, the quiet county seat of Wasco County, Oregon. A total of 751 people became ill, though none died. It was the largest outbreak of foodborne disease in the United States that year.

Public health and law enforcement officials were baffled. Their investigation found links to at least ten of the town's thirty-eight restaurants. Most of the restaurants where people had eaten before coming down with food poisoning had salad bars, but there was no common supplier. There didn't appear to be any pattern that connected all the cases—until the criminal investigation turned up the truth a year later.

Followers of Indian guru Bhagwan Shree Rajneesh had built a huge international headquarters and commune in Wasco County and were locked in a zoning dispute with the local government. So commune members came up with a plan: If they could make enough voters sick on election day, they could influence the outcome in their favor.

In September, two months before the election, they had a test run of their plan. They prepared cultures of *Salmonella typhimurium* bacteria in their secret lab on the commune, and then commune members poured the bacteria on food items in salad bars and, in some restaurants, into coffee creamers.

Two commune members eventually pleaded guilty and went to prison for the attack.

The Oregon attack taught us several hard lessons. It exposed our vulnerability to the deliberate contamination of food in public places. The salmonella culture used in the attack is easily obtained from raw foods bought in a grocery store, and it can be produced in large quantities with simple equipment and little expertise. Residents of The Dalles were fortunate that the cult didn't use a more lethal agent, such as botulinum toxin or even anthrax or tularemia.

The attack also underscored the need for health care providers and laboratories to closely cooperate and coordinate with local and state public health departments so that any future outbreaks can be detected more quickly.

And The Dalles case changed the way we look at public health emergencies. At the time, back in 1984, it never occurred to investigators that a group would deliberately contaminate food in several restaurants in an attempt to advance some twisted political or religious agenda.

Now we know that if a mysterious outbreak of infectious disease occurs that fits no known pattern and doesn't seem to have any common link, the possibility of intentional contamination must be considered, and law enforcement should be called in immediately to investigate.

mild, flulike illness. But the disease during pregnancy can lead to premature delivery, infection of the newborn, or even stillbirth. Infection of the fetus or newborn, however, can be prevented if antibiotics are given promptly to a pregnant woman.

Nine in ten people with listeriosis will require hospitalization, and one in five will die. Antibiotics are generally effective, but even with prompt treatment, some people with the infection will die. Those at highest risk are the elderly and persons with other serious medical problems.

Vibrio vulnificus

This bacterium normally survives in warm seawater. People usually contract the disease by eating contaminated seafood or having an open wound exposed to seawater.

The bacterium causes vomiting, diarrhea, and abdominal pain. Nine in ten people with the disease require hospitalization, and 39 percent die. The disease is treated with antibiotics. Top choices are doxycycline or ceftazidime.

How safe is our water supply?

Many people initially think water, since it comes so freely to each of our homes from a common community source, would be the ideal vehicle for the bioterrorist. Thankfully, it is not. In fact, although there has been some concern about our drinking water, as evidenced recently by increased security at our reservoirs, aqueducts, and dams, it is unlikely that a future bioterrorist attack would concentrate on our water supply for a variety of reasons.

First, most experts have concluded that it would be virtually impossible to cause widespread health problems by contaminating a major public water supply. Poisoning public drinking water would require truckloads of biochemical agents that would be difficult to produce and relatively easy to spot.

Every day, massive amounts of water are pumped from our reservoirs. Most of it goes for industrial and other purposes. Relatively little is actually consumed. So any biological agent put in the water at its source would be so diluted that it would have no effect by the time it came out of your faucet.

Second, drinking water from public sources in the United States is monitored constantly by sophisticated technology, and the presence of any contaminants would likely be detected. And if that's not enough, drinking water is typically aerated and heavily chlorinated. Chlorine protects drinking water from waterborne bacteria and neutralizes many biological agents.

And if water contamination were suspected, alternative water sources almost always could be tapped. For example, New York City has twenty reservoirs from which to choose.

It's possible, though still highly unlikely, that a contaminant could be placed in the system through a pipe downstream from the treatment plant. However, the water pressure is so great that even that would be extremely difficult. And the chlorine in the water would still probably offer protection.

So it is unlikely that the water supply is in danger. It certainly could not be the vehicle to deliver a weapon of mass destruction. However, the Environmental Protection Agency (EPA) is continually monitoring our risk to such an invasion.

WHO'S IN CHARGE OF DRINKING-WATER SAFETY?

Under a 1998 presidential directive, the EPA gained responsibility for protecting the nation's water supply from the threat of terrorism, including bioterrorism. Since then, the EPA has been working with utilities to assess vulnerabilities, guard against attack, and respond to an emergency.

In the wake of the September 11 attacks, the EPA formed the

Water Protection Task Force to develop comprehensive plans to protect our nation's water supply infrastructure, such as dams, treatment plants, and reservoirs.

The EPA also sent utilities information on steps they could take to protect their facilities and worked with the FBI to ask local law enforcement agencies to work closely with local water companies to beef up security.

IS BOTTLED WATER SAFER THAN TAP WATER?

Not necessarily. Keeping bottled water on hand as part of your disaster supply kit is probably a good idea. But in most cases, to the surprise of many except those marketing it, bottled water comes from a water source no different from the water. that comes out of your tap.

The fact is, public water is more closely regulated than bottled water. So the safety of bottled water depends on the safety and security precautions taken at the bottling plant. Tap water undergoes rigorous scrutiny and is protected by security measures approved by the EPA, state and local governments, and other organizations.

IF THE WATER SUPPLY IS SO SAFE, WHY WAS SECURITY INCREASED?

One of the lessons we learned from September 11 is that we must prepare as best we can for the unthinkable. The threat, though, isn't that someone will dump tons and tons of a biological agent into a reservoir when nobody's looking. It's that a sewage plant could be blown up along a river, contaminating the drinking water of millions of people downstream, or that a major dam could be brought down, unleashing floodwaters on cities in the way.

In these perilous times, heightened surveillance, security, and water-quality monitoring are clearly needed. And although the likelihood of poisoning a city's water supply is considered very small, the odds increase when you start talking about smaller targets—for example, a holding tank of treated water, a water system that serves a resort or an office building, or a bottling plant for water.

WHAT CAN I DO TO MAKE SURE MY WATER IS SAFE?

If you remain concerned, you might consider a home water-filtration system. I'll confess, I've used one for years. I have a system that serves my whole house in Washington, D.C., because I had some concerns about water quality when I first moved there. I also have a single filtration unit on the kitchen sink of my Nashville home. We drink tap water in both places.

My decision, though, has nothing to do with the threat of bioterrorism, and I'm certainly not saying everyone should run out and buy a filtration system. A single trip to just about any country overseas where you have to watch what you drink because the quality of public water is not so closely monitored quickly makes you realize how fortunate we are in this country to have such high-quality public drinking water.

That said, there may be some advantages to using water-treatment products. You might base your decision on local assessments of the water that actually comes to your house.

First, though, you should know that no current drinking-water treatment product can claim that it protects you from any biological or chemical agent. No tests have been done. That said, common products such as fine filtration systems, ultraviolet light (UV), reverse osmosis, and home distillation may offer some additional protection against biological or chemical agents, because they have been proven effective at screening out certain microorganisms.

WHAT IS AGROTERRORISM?

This is a word we all need to know and understand.

Agroterrorism is the use of biological weapons against animals or crops. To date, there have been no reported cases of agroterrorism in the United States. But there is a growing consensus that we could be particularly vulnerable.

Why? Because the technology required to stage a successful attack is relatively accessible. The resulting disruption to our economy could be significant. And we know that the Soviet Union during the Cold War and, more recently, Iraq developed antianimal and anticrop weapons as part of their bioweapons programs.

Unlike bioterrorism, the goal of agroterrorism would not be to cause widespread human death or illness. In fact, most of the biological agents likely to be used against animals or plants do not usually affect humans. The intent would be to radically disrupt another part of our infrastructure that we take for granted: our food supply. It would be to inspire terror by destroying something we depend on.

The economic impact of agroterrorism could be staggering. All we need to do is look at the costs of natural outbreaks. A 1996 outbreak of foot-and-mouth disease among swine in Taiwan resulted in almost 4 million hogs destroyed and losses to swine-related industries of $7 billion.

Britain's ongoing battle against mad cow disease has resulted in the destruction of more than 1.35 million head of cattle, at a cost of about $4.2 billion. On the basis of Britain's experience, it's estimated that the economic toll in the United States would be more than $15 billion if mad cow disease showed up on our shores.

U.S. animals and plants would be particularly susceptible to foreign diseases because they have not built up a natural resistance to them. And as agriculture has increasingly consolidated into large agribusinesses—some feedlots have as many as a hundred thousand animals—introducing a biological agent could quickly cause widespread infection.

   We are vulnerable.

HOW COULD AN AGROTERRORIST ATTACK BE CARRIED OUT AGAINST ANIMALS?

As we've seen, with bioterrorism and chemical weapons, launching a large-scale attack would require a fairly high degree of technical sophistication. An agroterrorism attack wouldn't.

   In fact, someone with just a basic understanding of microbiology could cultivate the virus that causes foot-and-mouth disease from an infected animal in another country, bring it into America, and spread it to a herd here by swabbing the virus into an animal's nose. It's no more complicated than that.

   Even a small outbreak would have significant consequences, since any outbreak of foot-and-mouth disease could trigger other countries to close their ports to U.S. animals and animal products—all from a single act of agricultural sabotage.

HOW COULD AN AGROTERRORIST ATTACK BE CARRIED OUT AGAINST PLANTS?

Most crop diseases don't kill plants. They dramatically decrease their yield or diminish the quality of the plant. Just as viruses are the greatest threats to animals, fungi are plants' most dangerous enemy.

   Deliberately spreading crop diseases is considerably more difficult than spreading a virus through a herd, though. For one thing, most of the biological agents likely to be used against crops are sensitive to environmental factors such as temperature, humidity, and sunlight. Plus, they don't travel airborne as fast or far as animal diseases.

One major obstacle terrorists would have to overcome is weather variables. To illustrate the difficulty, consider that in 1999, top university plant pathologists, armed with a particularly virulent strain of late blight disease and test potatoes that were susceptible to the disease, were unable to create an epidemic for research purposes. The reason: drought.

However, the mere fact that a crop is exposed to a known biological agent may be enough to cause other countries to cut off imports, causing a huge ripple effect through the economy.

WHAT IS MAD COW DISEASE?

It's actually bovine spongiform encephalopathy, or BSE, a brain-wasting disease that has been found in cattle in eighteen countries. There has never been a case of mad cow disease in the United States, and a government-funded study recently concluded that there is little risk of American cattle contracting the incurable disease.

Still, it is a major concern because humans can contract a form of the disease by eating tainted meat, and it is always fatal. Variant Creutzfeldt-Jakob disease (vCJD), the form that strikes humans, has killed more than a hundred Europeans, mostly in Britain.

The disease was first diagnosed in British cattle fifteen years ago. Since then, there have been more than 180,000 cases of BSE reported, all but about 1,500 of those in Britain. And the actual number of infected animals is estimated at about 1 million, although the number of cases has been steadily declining since 1993.

When the government in Britain announced in 1996 that eating contaminated meat was linked to the human form of mad cow disease, the $880-million-a-year British beef industry became worthless almost overnight. It took two years and an extensive, government-funded public relations campaign for the industry to begin to recover.

The disease is believed to spread among cattle by infected feed containing meat-and-bonemeal, a protein supplement made from ground-up parts of cows. The U.S. banned meat-and-bonemeal and other mammal-based animal protein in cattle feed in 1997. And European beef is banned in the United States because of concerns over mad cow disease.

Scientists believe that an aberrant protein, known as a prion, causes mad cow disease. Prion diseases are not unheard of in the United States. Although no cases of mad cow have ever been reported here, about three hundred cases of prion diseases occur in the United States each year.

About one in every million Americans is struck with classical Creutzfeldt-Jakob disease, which also can be spread by surgical instruments used in brain operations. Experts are concerned that the deadly vCJD may be more infectious than the classical form we've seen here, and that it may spread though blood or other ways. That's why many U.S. blood banks won't accept blood from people who have stayed in Britain for more than three months or other parts of Europe for more than six months since 1980.

WHAT IS FOOT-AND-MOUTH DISEASE?

Because they both broke out in Britain, many people in the United States confuse foot-and-mouth disease with mad cow disease. But they are two very different and unrelated diseases. The only thing they have in common is a devastating impact on the British economy.

Unlike mad cow disease, foot-and-mouth—or hoof-and-mouth, as it's sometimes known—poses little danger to people, even if they eat the meat of infected animals. It only strikes cloven-hoofed animals like sheep, cows, goats, and pigs. And foot-and-mouth is rarely fatal.

But it is highly contagious and debilitates infected animals, leaving them unable to grow or produce milk. Last year's outbreak in

Britain led the United States to ban imports of animals and animal products from the European Union. Imagine if this were to happen to the United States!

The ban is expected to cost European exporters $400 million a year. But the economic toll on Britain is already far higher. It's estimated that the cost to British farming, tourism, and other industries will exceed $3 billion. And the effects on British agriculture will be felt for years. More than 3.5 million animals have been slaughtered in an effort to stop the spread of the virus.

The problem is that the virus is extremely resourceful. It can spread from pigs to sheep to other animals. It can spread through farm machinery. And it can spread through airborne particles. In 1981, foot-and-mouth cases showed up on the Isle of Wight just three days after an outbreak in Brittany, France. The most likely explanation is that the virus traveled 175 miles across the English Channel through the air.

WHAT OTHER DISEASES POSE THE GREATEST AGROTERROR THREAT AGAINST ANIMALS?

The International Office of Epizootics represents 155 member nations and is responsible for setting animal health standards on which international trade restrictions are based. The organization has compiled a list of the diseases that could spread rapidly and cause serious economic and public health problems. An outbreak of any one of these diseases would likely result in an international export embargo.

In addition to foot-and-mouth disease, others on the list include:

- Vesicular stomatitis. Spread by insects and direct contact, such as shared feed and water troughs; affects cattle, swine, and horses; found in the United States, Mexico, Canada, the

Caribbean, and Central and South America; humans can get a version resembling the flu.

- Swine vesicular disease. Spread by eating infected meat; affects swine; found in Hong Kong, Japan, and Europe; can cause flulike symptoms in humans.

- Rinderpest. Also known as cattle plague. Spread by airborne droplets and direct contact with animal fluids; affects cattle, sheep, and goats; found in Africa, the Middle East, and Asia; no effect on humans.

- Contagious bovine pleuropneumonia. Spread by inhaling droplets of animal fluids; affects cattle; found in Asia, central Africa, Spain, and Portugal; no effect on humans.

- Lumpy skin disease. Spread by insects; affects cattle; found in Africa; no effect on humans.

- Rift Valley fever. Spread by insects, especially mosquitoes, and direct contact with blood or tissue; affects sheep and cattle; found in Africa; humans are very susceptible—disease can be fatal, though a vaccine is available.

- Bluetongue. Spread by insects; affects sheep and cattle; found in U.S., Africa, and Europe; no effect on humans.

- African swine fever. Spread by ticks, eating infected meat, direct contact, and airborne aerosols within buildings; affects swine; found in Africa, the Iberian Peninsula, and Sardinia; no effect on humans.

- Classical swine fever. Also known as hog cholera. Spread by direct contact with animal fluids and indirect contact on shoes, clothing, and equipment; affects swine; found in Africa, Asia, South and Central America, and parts of Europe; no effect on humans.

- Highly pathogenic avian influenza. Also known as fowl plague. Spread by direct contact and through the air; affects chickens and turkeys; found worldwide; rarely affects humans, but 1997 Hong Kong epidemic killed six.

- Newcastle disease. Spread by direct contact with animal feces and other secretions and contaminated feed, water, equipment, human clothing; affects poultry and wild birds; found worldwide; sometimes causes brief conjunctivitis in humans after extensive exposure.

WHAT DISEASES POSE THE GREATEST AGROTERROR THREAT AGAINST PLANTS?

When the Soviet Union and Iraq developed biological agents to use against crops, they targeted primarily those that would harm cereals: wheat, barley, and rye. The most likely fungi to be used against the cereal crops are stem rust of wheat, stripe rust of cereals, and powdery mildew of cereals. All are spread by airborne spores.

Against corn, the bacteria that cause corn blight are at the top of the list. They would be spread by spraying.

The fungi that cause rice blast and rice brown-spot disease are likely to be used against rice. Both would be spread by airborne spores. The bacteria that cause rice blight, spread by spraying, also could be used against rice.

Late blight, the disease that caused the potato famine in Ireland in 1845, would be of chief concern for potato crops. It's a fungus, spread by airborne spores.

11

A NATION PREPARED
Safeguarding Our Future

To overcome the threat of the intentional use of germs against us, we must call upon all the resources available to us. As citizens, we have the responsibility to insist that our government, both local and federal, is responding appropriately to the new challenges of bioterrorism.

In the preceding chapters, we have concentrated on what we as individuals need to know and can do to protect ourselves and our loved ones. Knowledge is power as we deal with bioterrorism. But true success requires a government that is also prepared.

As a nation, we need a cohesive, comprehensive, three-pronged approach to prevent, prepare for, and respond to any future bioterrorist attacks. Fortunately, we're not starting from scratch. A lot of work has been done in recent years to recognize and begin to deal with the threat we face.

More than three years ago, as chairman of the Senate Public Health Subcommittee, I held a series of in-depth hearings on the ability of our nation's public health system—at the local, state, and national levels—to respond to public health threats. In one hearing we focused on bioterrorism in the United States, and it quickly became clear that the threat was real, that it was increasing, and that we, as a nation, were not fully prepared to meet it.

In the truly bipartisan manner that such an important issue deserves, I worked closely with Sen. Edward M. Kennedy to draft and pass the Public Health Threats and Emergencies Act of 2000. The original legislation, enacted almost a year before the September 11 attacks, provided the framework to coordinate the response of federal, state, and local agencies to a bioterrorist attack.

It also provided a blueprint for strengthening the capabilities of those entities and organizations in your community—and in communities all across the country—that will be called upon to respond immediately if a bioterrorist attack occurs. These include public health agencies and laboratories, hospitals and other health care facilities, and the emergency personnel you will call and who will be responding to your calls.

But as often happens, the legislation was never fully funded. Our hope was to gradually and carefully implement the program so that over a decade, each state—and through each state, every community—would become fully prepared.

Now we know that we cannot wait. Our time line must be accelerated for the safety and health of your family. We must act now to ensure that our public health system is able to respond to what you and your family will need in the event a bioterrorist assault occurs in your neighborhood. And that means we must provide adequate resources to communities around the country so that they can use them in their own way to meet their own particular needs, rather than providing a one-size-fits-all solution from Washington.

For these reasons, I once again joined with Senator Kennedy to cosponsor the Bioterrorism Preparedness Act of 2001, which builds on the foundation we laid two years ago with the Public Health Threats and Emergencies Act and points the way to a safer, more secure future. More than two dozen of my Senate colleagues made major contributions to this legislation. Sens. Judd Gregg, Susan Collins, Pat Roberts, Chris Dodd, and Mike DeWine deserve special recognition.The legislation not only fills the gaps in our public infrastructure that were defined so clearly in the anthrax attacks in the fall of 2001 but also addresses the areas of food safety and agroterror that have been sorely neglected in the past.

WHAT CAN WE DO TO PREVENT FUTURE BIOTERRORIST ATTACKS?

There are several things we need to do. Improving our intelligence-gathering capabilities so that we can thwart planned attacks before they happen obviously is extremely important. And our government is doing that. Who has the smallpox virus? Which rogue nations have active offensive-bioweapons programs under way?

Our war against the Taliban in Afghanistan was not only to bring to justice those responsible for the unspeakable attacks of September 11. Part of what we sought to accomplish was to wipe out their ability to stage future attacks, including bioterrorist attacks.

We know that Iraq had a substantial bioweapons program in the years leading up to the Gulf War. Working with the United Nations, we're closely monitoring what happens there to ensure that that technology is never used.

Making sure the expertise and technology developed in the former Soviet Union's massive offensive bioweapons program isn't made available to terrorists or rogue nations is another preventive step we are currently taking. Where are the Russian scientists now?

Here at home, we need to gain tighter control over those biological agents that could be used to harm our people. We also need to greatly enhance our food safety program by giving the Food and Drug Administration (FDA) the additional resources and authority it needs to do its job.

WHAT ARE WE DOING TO MINIMIZE THE LINGERING THREAT CREATED BY THE SOVIET BIOWEAPONS PROGRAM?

Currently, anywhere from eleven to seventeen countries have biological weapons programs, including Russia, which has the largest and most sophisticated facilities, many of whose locations are unknown.

We know that, beginning in 1980, the Soviets embarked on a successful offensive bioweapons program that produced tons of smallpox virus for use in bombs and intercontinental ballistic missiles. We know that the Soviets also manufactured plague for use in weapons and researched other biological agents, including all those discussed in the chapters in this book, such as anthrax, tularemia, and botulinum toxin.

With the breakup of the Soviet Union, there remains a real concern that all of that expertise and technology could fall into the hands of rogue nations or terrorist organizations. More than seven thousand scientists worked in the bioweapons program during the 1980s. Many of them are now unemployed or working in less lucrative or challenging fields, and there is the very real concern that they could offer to sell their services and their technological know-how to the highest bidder.

So under the Department of Defense's Former Soviet Union Threat Reduction program, the federal government is taking steps to ensure that that doesn't happen by assisting the republics of the former Soviet Union, and in part by directly subsidizing these scientists. In 2001, we spent about $511 million to:

- Provide contracts or grants to aid the elimination and the safe and secure transportation and storage of biological, chemical, nuclear, and other weapons.

- Establish programs to prevent the proliferation of weapons, weapons components, and weapon-related technology and expertise.

- Support programs that train former Soviet defense and military personnel for nonmilitary work, and protect weapons, weapons components, weapons technology, and expertise.

It is in our country's best interests to keep Soviet scientists and technology off the black market. This program is designed to do just that. I am hopeful that the special relationship that exists between President Bush and Russian president Vladimir V. Putin will lead to new opportunities for greater cooperation and more collaboration to reduce common threats.

WHAT CAN WE DO TO MAKE SURE BIOLOGICAL AGENTS LIKE ANTHRAX DON'T WIND UP IN THE WRONG HANDS?

Many industry and law enforcement personnel have been surprised to discover how widespread is the distribution of bacteria and germs that could be used as bioweapons. Anthrax exists in laboratories of research, academic, and military institutions all over the country.

Federal law already regulates the transfer of dangerous biological agents. But we need to do more. The secretary of health and human services should come up with a list of biological agents and toxins that pose the greatest threat to public health, and the government should more aggressively regulate possession, use, and transfer of those agents. Violators should face stiff civil penalties, as well as criminal sanctions.

HOW DO WE MAKE IT MORE DIFFICULT FOR BIOTERRORISTS TO ATTACK OUR FOOD SUPPLY?

We absolutely must do more to ensure the safety of our food.

Our ports are particularly vulnerable. We currently have 175

FDA inspectors to cover more than three hundred ports where food is brought into this country. Clearly, we need to hire more inspectors, and we need to grant them the authority they need to do their job right.

In addition to hiring more inspectors, we should allow the FDA to use qualified employees from other agencies to help conduct food inspections. And any domestic or foreign plant that makes or processes food for use in the United States should have to register with the FDA so we will know where the food is coming from.

In addition, importers should be required to notify the FDA about their country of origin and what food they're bringing in. And to prevent "port shopping," the FDA needs to be able to mark food shipments denied entry at one port so the ships don't just sail a few hundred miles to gain entry at another port.

To prevent possible contamination of our food, the FDA should be given what is called detention authority. Instead of having to wait for people to die or become seriously ill to issue a food recall, the FDA should be able to detain a food shipment it believes poses a serious health threat to people or animals. Detention authority would ensure that the food isn't distributed to your dinner table while the FDA is spending time going to court to obtain a seizure order.

We also need to give the FDA the tools it needs to trace the source and distribution of any food that poses a health threat. We can do that by simply requiring those who manufacture, process, pack, transport, distribute, receive, hold, or import food to maintain proper records for the FDA's inspection. It may be more record keeping, but it will mean that we can quickly identify any risk to your health.

And anyone who engages in a pattern of trying to import food that presents a health threat to people or animals should be barred from doing business here. Period.

As you can see, we've not done as good a job as we should have in giving the FDA the tools it needs so our families can rest assured that our food supply will be safe. Now is the time to act.

SO TELL US HONESTLY, SENATOR, ARE WE PREPARED FOR A BIOTERRORIST ATTACK?

Clearly, America is not ready to meet this deadly threat. We can send an e-mail message across the globe in the blink of an eye, but the public health agency in your community upon which you will depend might not even have equipment as basic as a fax machine. And the success of public health agencies in fighting infectious disease or bioterrorism depends on rapid communication. Scientists have deciphered the entire DNA sequence of the human genetic code, but many public health laboratories cannot conduct basic tests to identify deadly microbes rapidly and accurately.

In a disease emergency, swift action is essential to keep a local outbreak from becoming a national epidemic. Lost hours mean lost lives. Every moment counts.

Today we remain highly vulnerable. But I want to make one thing clear. It's not that we're *un*prepared. It's that we're *under*-prepared. We can't lose sight of the fact that in our federal, state, local, and private health systems, we have all the pieces we need to wage an effective defense against bioterrorism.

We just need to coordinate those pieces in a seamless way. And we need to commit the resources necessary to hire well-trained epidemiologists, upgrade our laboratory capabilities, and improve our communications systems. This can be done. But it will take your support. You must call for it.

Before coming to the Senate, I was a heart transplant surgeon. Daily, I witnessed how hospitals, personnel, laboratories, and health systems across the country could rapidly communicate with each other and work together in a seamless, coordinated, efficient way to carry off each and every transplant. We need to better apply these same principles to combat bioterrorism. Coordination and communication—those are the keys.

The gaps we now see in our public health system are the result of twenty years of benign neglect and underinvestment. We've already begun to correct the problems. But we still have a lot of work to do. And we must do it now. Success will depend on the support of individual Americans who take time to understand where the gaps are and then actively call for filling the gaps.

IF THE ODDS OF A BIOTERRORIST ATTACK ARE LOW, DOES IT REALLY MAKE SENSE TO SPEND BILLIONS OF DOLLARS TO PREPARE FOR IT?

First, investing in upgrading our public health system makes sense *even if we never experience another bioterrorist attack.* And I pray we won't. In a sense, the fundamental health issue here is infectious disease. Bioterrorism, when you come right down to it, is simply the deliberate attempt to spread infectious diseases.

But we're going to have to deal with these and similar diseases whether they're spread by terrorists or occur naturally. This is an important point: Any improvements we make in our ability to respond to a bioterrorist attack will serve the very valuable dual purpose of better preparing us to handle all infectious and communicable diseases—from the flu that strikes millions and kills thousands each year, to the food poisoning that annually hospitalizes over 300,000, to the new emerging infectious diseases caused by antibiotic-resistant organisms, to HIV/AIDS, which infects more than a million Americans right now.

Infectious diseases are diseases caused by living organisms, such as bacteria or viruses. As we have seen, the biological agents we face aren't new. Anthrax, smallpox, the plague—they've been around for centuries. And as we've also seen, there's nothing new about mankind's attempts to turn these infectious diseases against others. We're just dealing with a higher level of sophistication and technology in the way it's done.

In the last century, modern medicine made significant strides toward freeing us from the threat of many infectious diseases that had plagued humanity through the ages. We actually eradicated natural outbreaks of smallpox. That's an amazing accomplishment, a remarkable public health victory that has saved the lives of millions of children, women, and men.

Through the development of vaccines and antibiotics over the past sixty years, it appeared we were on the verge of winning the war against infectious disease. In the 1970s even the surgeon general of the United States said that we would see the end of infectious diseases as a significant problem. But in underdeveloped nations around the world, horrible infectious diseases such as Ebola continued to claim lives. And in developed countries, as antibiotic usage grew, new antibiotic-resistant organisms began to emerge.

As we move into the twenty-first century, the reality is that infectious diseases are still the second leading cause of death worldwide. Worldwide, HIV/AIDS claims three million lives a year, tuberculosis two million, and malaria one million. And here in the United States, infections remain the third leading cause of death.

Meanwhile, the world, because of advances in transportation, is a much smaller place. And germs know no borders. Early last year, I had a meeting with U2's lead singer, Bono. He has been very active in the global fight against AIDS and other infectious diseases. As he said in that meeting, "An infectious disease is just one cheap airplane seat away from any major city in the world."

Sadly, the same can be said of bioterrorism.

WHAT ARE THE KEY AREAS IN PUBLIC HEALTH THAT WE NOW KNOW NEED TO BE IMPROVED?

As we learned from the anthrax-related events last fall, we must improve training, communication, and coordination between the various parts of our public health system.

Public health offices at the local and state levels have been underfunded and understaffed for years, in part because they have not had a very effective constituency arguing for their importance in Washington, D.C. The quickest and most effective way to fill the gaps uncovered by the anthrax threats is to immediately expand federal grants to allow states and local public health offices to address the challenges that face them.

WHY IS TRAINING FOR THOSE ON THE FRONT LINE OF RESPONSE SO IMPORTANT?

If a bioterrorist attack occurs, those on the front lines won't only be firefighters and police officers. They will be doctors and nurses in emergency rooms and private practices, and epidemiologists and lab technicians in public and private laboratories.

Their ability to quickly and correctly recognize diseases with which they have had little or, more commonly, no direct experience—anthrax, smallpox, plague, and the other agents we have discussed—will largely determine how many people fall seriously ill or die.

We need to better educate medical professionals about infections and organisms that could be used as bioweapons. Our intelligence community has identified which ones those are. And a better understanding of, and more research into, infectious diseases generally would better prepare us to reduce their toll of death and sickness.

WHAT CAN BE DONE TO IMPROVE COMMUNICATIONS AND COORDINATION?

We need to improve communication among the various clinical facilities, laboratories, and personnel in your community. We must also strengthen communication between the local public health system and the state and federal governmental bodies. The flow of information needs to be seamless.

Just after September 11, for example, the Centers for Disease

Control and Prevention (CDC) sent an alert on bioterrorism to all state health officials. A week later, the alert still had not reached many local emergency rooms—which, in all likelihood, would be the first line of defense if such an attack occurred. That's inexcusable in this day of on-line access, especially when it comes to our safety.

If we're at war, the soldiers on the front line need to be the first to know that an attack is coming—not the last. And our hospitals must plan for how they would meet such a threat. Before September 11, for example, only one in five U.S. hospitals had bioterrorism-preparedness plans in place.

One of the most effective things we can do is to ensure that we develop and maintain an integrated, state-of-the-art, real-time computer communications system that efficiently links local, state, and federal public health officials and private facilities, researchers, and providers and allows them to share information with each other.

Communications between doctors and public health agencies, and between public health agencies and the government, also are lacking. One in five public health offices does not have e-mail. In this high-tech age, many public health offices still collect information on disease outbreaks by having doctors send in postcards.

Disease surveillance is a crucial part of the system. If ten people go to ten different doctors or hospitals with symptoms of a particular microorganism, we need to be able to make that connection faster than by sending a postcard through the mail. As we've seen time and time again in this book, every moment counts, and a fast response is literally a matter of life and death when it comes to a bioterrorist attack.

The first line of defense, as I've said before, is alert, well-trained doctors and nurses. But this is an area where computers can help tremendously. There are data-collection systems that can analyze medical records and, in a heartbeat, make connections that people would probably miss. New York City, for instance, keeps hourly tabs on the sale of antidiarrhea medication. The city also tracks 911 calls for reports of respiratory problems, which has proven to be a fast and accurate indicator of flu outbreaks.

We also need to improve coordination between the agencies and departments—federal, state, and local—that will respond if there is a bioterrorist attack. This should be accomplished by designating an assistant secretary for emergency preparedness at the Department of Health and Human Services who would be responsible for coordinating all emergency preparedness efforts, including response to bioterrorist threats and attacks.

And we need to bring together the leaders of key federal departments on an ongoing basis, including Health and Human Services, Justice, Defense, Agriculture, and the Federal Emergency Management Agency, to coordinate bioterrorism countermeasures, from research on likely biological agents to response to an actual attack. Our federal departments should not duplicate each other's efforts. They should complement and supplement each other.

As we all witnessed during the anthrax scare last fall, we must improve and streamline our methods of communicating with the public. As part of this strategy, the federal government and the states should designate in advance a lead spokesperson who is able to reliably and accurately convey vital information to the public in the event of an attack. We also should provide uniform, up-to-date information through an official federal website and explore other means of rapidly communicating accurate information to the public.

The bioterrorist events of last fall underscored the critical need for—and the value of—accurate and timely information. It leads to a more responsive citizenry and a calmer nation. When we don't know, we should say, "We just don't know yet."

DO THE INTERESTS OF CHILDREN OR OTHER VULNERABLE
POPULATIONS REQUIRE A SPECIAL FOCUS BY OUR GOVERNMENT?

As we develop plans to deal with the threat of bioterrorism, we must specifically focus on the needs of children and other vulnerable populations. As we've seen, children may be at particular risk during a biological or chemical attack. Many of the vaccines and antibiotics we would use have not been studied adequately in children. While there clearly is much more we need to learn about the impact of various biological agents, our knowledge about how they affect children and how to treat children lags even further behind.

Moreover, as suggested by the anthrax attacks of last fall, the immune system of elderly individuals may be sufficiently different to increase their susceptibility to certain microorganisms.

WHAT CAN STATES DO TO BE PREPARED FOR A BIOTERRORIST ATTACK?

Much of what needs to be done is outlined above in terms of better planning and enhanced capabilities. But states also need to reexamine their basic public health laws to make sure they are updated to deal with current threats. At the request of the CDC, the Center for Law and the Public's Health in 2001 drafted a model piece of legislation called the State Emergency Health Powers Act. This model law identifies areas on which states should focus to prepare for the threat of bioterrorism, as well as other public health threats and emergencies.

It calls for states to create a public health emergency planning commission charged with developing a comprehensive plan to cover all aspects of a public health emergency, including how to:

- Notify and communicate with the public during an emergency

- Centralize coordination between state, federal, and local agencies

FROM A DARK WINTER
TO A BRIGHT FUTURE

In the past two years, we have held two military exercises to test our readiness to respond to a bioterrorist attack. We must heed the lessons learned from those exercises.

TOPOFF, short for "top officials," was held in March 2000 and simulated a plague outbreak in Denver. Within a week, the hypothetical plague had spread to other states, and even as far away as England and Japan. By the end of the exercise, the number of sick and dead couldn't be determined because of conflicting reports, but the range was 3,700 to more than 4,000 cases, with 950 to more than 2,000 deaths.

Among the key results that we can—and must—build on were:

- It was unclear who was in charge. Conference calls, some of which included fifty to a hundred people from various federal, state, and local agencies who had never previously met or worked together, bogged down in indecision.

- Communications broke down. Information on such crucial issues as how many confirmed or suspected cases of plague had broken out would not have been available to decision makers. Hospital officials couldn't reach health department and other officials because they weren't answering their phones: they were at operations centers, or taking part in conference calls, or were just too busy managing the crisis.

- Delivery and distribution of antibiotics to hospitals was delayed. Local supplies were exhausted early in the crisis. When antibiotics were sent from the National Pharmaceutical Stockpile, they sat at the airport for hours while plastic bags were bought and delivered, and then one person counted out the pills and put them into the bags.

- Health care facilities were swamped. Within the first twenty-four hours of the exercise, hospitals had exceeded their capacity. And much of the demand came from "worried well"—people who didn't have the plague but were afraid that they might.

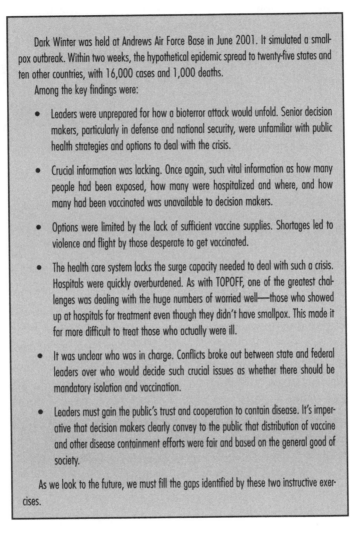

Dark Winter was held at Andrews Air Force Base in June 2001. It simulated a smallpox outbreak. Within two weeks, the hypothetical epidemic spread to twenty-five states and ten other countries, with 16,000 cases and 1,000 deaths.

Among the key findings were:

• Leaders were unprepared for how a bioterror attack would unfold. Senior decision makers, particularly in defense and national security, were unfamiliar with public health strategies and options to deal with the crisis.

• Crucial information was lacking. Once again, such vital information as how many people had been exposed, how many were hospitalized and where, and how many had been vaccinated was unavailable to decision makers.

• Options were limited by the lack of sufficient vaccine supplies. Shortages led to violence and flight by those desperate to get vaccinated.

• The health care system lacks the surge capacity needed to deal with such a crisis. Hospitals were quickly overburdened. As with TOPOFF, one of the greatest challenges was dealing with the huge numbers of worried well—those who showed up at hospitals for treatment even though they didn't have smallpox. This made it far more difficult to treat those who actually were ill.

• It was unclear who was in charge. Conflicts broke out between state and federal leaders over who would decide such crucial issues as whether there should be mandatory isolation and vaccination.

• Leaders must gain the public's trust and cooperation to contain disease. It's imperative that decision makers clearly convey to the public that distribution of vaccine and other disease containment efforts were fair and based on the general good of society.

As we look to the future, we must fill the gaps identified by these two instructive exercises.

- Provide essential emergency needs, including medical supplies, drugs, vaccines, food, shelter, and beds

- Keep courts operating smoothly, and even provide for emergency judges in case quarantining is required

- Safely evacuate, feed, and house people in an emergency, if needed

- Train health care providers to diagnose and treat infectious diseases

- Develop guidelines for vaccinations

Once the plan is in place, it would grant the governor of a state broad powers to declare a public health emergency when there is an imminent threat or outbreak of infectious disease, whether caused by bioterrorism or occurring naturally.

The governor would have the authority to use all of the resources of state government to respond, including transferring personnel from other state departments and agencies to help where needed. The National Guard also could be called to active duty.

In the military modeling exercises TOPOFF and Dark Winter, we saw the problems we could face with inadequate personnel and supplies. We also saw the potential for civil unrest if the public isn't clear about who's in charge and why actions are being taken.

The model legislation spells these things out clearly. Rationing of vaccines or other supplies, if necessary, would be controlled by public health officials. Preference could expressly be given to health care providers, disaster response teams, and mortuary staff. Public health officials would have broader powers to compel individuals to undergo examination, medical testing, vaccination, or treatment.

As part of those broader powers, officials would have more options to quarantine those who are determined to pose a serious threat to public health.Several steps would be required to make that determination, as officials must balance the individual's rights against dangers to public health. And protections must be built in to ensure patient confidentiality.

Enactment of this general type of legislation would go a long way toward ensuring that we are adequately prepared for the threat of bioterrorism. But governors and other officials need to use forbearance and caution in exercising some of the sweeping powers that would be provided by such laws. And remember that legal authorities alone are no substitute for ongoing training and adequate public health resources. I also want to stress that this legislation is needed to deal with *all* health risks posed by infectious diseases.

HOW CAN WE BE SURE THERE WILL BE SUFFICIENT PERSONNEL AND SUPPLIES TO RESPOND TO A BIOTERRORIST ATTACK?

As the military exercises clearly demonstrated, our health care system is not capable of handling what's called the surge that would be created by a large-scale biological disaster. In some hospitals now, a flu outbreak can overtax resources.

I advocate expanding federal response capabilities by formally establishing a national disaster medical response system. This group of volunteers could be called up by the secretary of health and human services to respond to a public health emergency, much like the National Guard is mobilized for disasters. And I favor granting these volunteers the same full liability protection, reemployment rights, and other legal safeguards that are given the National Guard.

We also need to increase resources for the National Pharmaceutical Stockpile so that we are fully prepared for any attack. This valuable national resource is ready today to ship at a moment's notice truckloads of lifesaving vaccines and medical supplies and equipment so that they arrive within twelve hours anywhere in the United States. The pharmaceutical stockpile was used for the first time in response to the September 11 attacks in New York City.

There are still infectious diseases for which we don't have vaccines or treatments, so we need to devote more resources to developing them. Because early testing on human beings is obviously out of the question, the FDA needs to come up with reasonable guidelines for the approval of potentially lifesaving drugs based on animal testing. And to make sure we have sufficient supplies of vaccines, I favor having the federal government enter into long-term contracts with suppliers guaranteeing the purchase of a certain quantity at a fixed price. To encourage participation, the private sector needs some certainty in terms of market. New public-private partnerships are the only way to speedily address the development of new tests, vaccines, and treatments to combat the increasing threat of bioterrorism.

We also should provide limited antitrust relief to drug companies so they can use resources wisely to quickly produce needed vaccines and drugs. And we need to extend reasonable limits on liability exposure so that these countermeasures can be produced at a reasonable cost. Reasonable liability protection is an important component of the public-private partnership and is the only way that our country can deliver in a timely way the vaccines that will protect you and your family.

ARE YOU OPTIMISTIC THAT WE CAN MEET THE CHALLENGES THAT LIE AHEAD?

Absolutely! We know the challenges. They were not completely unknown before the anthrax attacks of 2001, but they were not nearly so clearly defined. We now call upon the best in the American spirit that exists in communities all across this great land.

As Americans, we have always looked to the future. With knowledge of what to do, we know that we can be prepared. With an understanding of what to do in the event of an attack, we will be protected. With recognition that we have underinvested in our public health infrastructure, we will call for improvement.

And with the most powerful private and public research and scientific communities in the world, the synergies of partnerships in addressing the threats before us will lead to success. Partnerships between federal and local governments, partnerships among the federal agencies, and partnerships among local public health entities are being established to the benefit of all.

In the coming months, we will continue to assess where we are and what we need to do to be fully prepared. Our benchmark will be the changes that we incorporate to ensure that each day, we are more able to respond because we have thought about our vulnerabilities, assessed appropriate actions, and taken steps to ensure that the next biological attack will be met with the full force of a coordinated, well-developed, expertly trained disaster response team.

Every one of us is a key player on that team.

INTERNET RESOURCES

For the most reliable, updated information on bioterrorism—information you can trust—there are several outstanding websites. These are the ones I have found most helpful.

American Medical Association:
  www.ama-assn.org
American Psychological Association:
  http://helping.apa.org/daily/ptguidelines.html
Association for Professionals in Infection Control and
  Epidemiology: www.apic.org/bioterror/
Center for the Study of Bioterrorism and Emerging Infections,
  St. Louis University:
  www.slu.edu/colleges/sph/bioterrorism/index.html
Centers for Disease Control and Prevention (CDC):
  www.bt.cdc.gov/ (This should be a primary reference.)
Johns Hopkins University:
  www.hopkins-biodefense.org/
State Public Health locator:
  www.statepublichealth.org/directory.php (This is a great portal
  that allows you to quickly find good local information.)
U.S. Army Medical Research Institute of Infectious Diseases
  (USAMRIID): www.usamriid.army.mil/

U.S. Postal Service:
www.usps.com/news/2001/press/serviceup dates.htm
U.S. Senator Bill Frist, M.D.:
http://frist.senate.gov
World Health Organization (WHO):
www.who.int/home-page/

INDEX

Main entries for names of diseases are in bold type.

ABOUT THE AUTHOR

First elected to the U.S. Senate in 1994, Senator Bill Frist, M.D. (R-Tenn.), is the first practicing physician to become a U.S. senator since 1928. In addition to performing more than 150 heart and lung transplant procedures, Senator Frist has written more than one hundred articles, chapters, and abstracts on medical research as well as several books. He is ranking member of the Subcommittee on Public Health, serves in the Senate leadership, and was named one of two congressional representatives to the United Nations General Assembly. Senator Frist and his wife, Karyn, have three sons.